BETWEEN LITTLE ROCK AND A HARD PLACE

The new gay/ lesbian/ bisexual struggle for national political POWER

Tommi Avicolli Mecca

Williams *PUBLISHING*

Thank You

I would like to thank the following individuals for making this book possible: first and foremost Richard Labonte at A Different Light Bookstore in San Francisco, the kindest man I've ever met; Norman Laurila, co-owner of A Different Light, for good advice; Gregory King at Human Rights Campaign Fund and Robin Kane at National Gay and Lesbian Task Force for their invaluable research assistance; my dear friend Winchester for always believing in me; my friend Ted Tallase for being there when this task became overwhelming; and Simeon White for the political discussions.

Acknowledgements

To *San Francisco Bay Times* Production Manager Brendan Ward for the title of this book, which was his title for an article I wrote on Clinton for the paper during the primary, and to the *Washington Blade* for its excellent coverage of the presidential race.

a famiglia mia

(you know who you are)

Table of Contents

Note to Readers

I will use the word *queer* interchangeably with gay/lesbian/bisexual/transgendered in this book for many reasons. Primarily, I want to reclaim a word that has been used against me and my brothers and sisters. If we use it in a positive sense, then all the hatemongers in the universe have no more power to hurt us with that word.

Queer is used today to encompass all of us in the sexual minority community: gay men, lesbians, bisexuals, transsexuals, transvestites, leather folks, and so forth. As a noun, it is less cumbersome than the entire laundry list of names to describe us.

It's also a powerful word, an in-your-face word, something non-apologetic and loud. Not clinical sounding like homosexual, or frivolous like gay.

I know that many in my community do not like the word queer; in fact, they cringe at its sound. They don't see how empowering it is to reclaim it from the homophobes. I understand their pain at hearing it. But I ask that they understand my need to take back a word that was used against me for far too many years.

Introduction

Watching Our Backs

A LOT OF PEOPLE were surprised in September 1991 when
California Governor Pete Wilson vetoed AB 101, the
state's gay/lesbian rights bill.

Not me.

You have to be crazy to trust a politician. Or just off
the ship from Alpha Centauri. Politicians deceive. Frequently, they out and out lie. Not many people would
disagree. Everyone knows a politician will say anything,
project any image necessary, to gain your confidence, to
win your vote.

Remember California Senator Dianne Feinstein
when she was mayor of San Francisco? She succeeded
George Moscone who was gunned down along with out
queer supervisor Harvey Milk by homophobic supervisor Dan White. Feinstein touted herself (and still does)
as a friend to the queer community. Her credentials were
flawless: she was Milk's friend; she was Moscone's friend;
she was a liberal.

And yet she vetoed domestic partners legislation,
which would have given the lovers of gay/lesbian/bi-
sexual/transgendered San Francisco city employees the

same benefits as their heterosexual counterparts. She said at the time that she was worried about the price tag.

As if rights should ever have a price tag. Believe me, if that were the case, the only folks in this country who'd have any rights at all (including the power to vote) would be those who had them originally: white wealthy male landowners.

If you can't trust the liberals, who can you trust? Certainly not the conservatives. But at least with a conservative, you know where you stand. With liberals, you have to watch your back all the time. You think I'm joking?

Another case in point: Former San Francisco Supervisor Dick Hongisto used to be a liberal. He stood up for queers a long time ago, back before it was popular to do so. He spoke at gay/lesbian functions; he would have kissed gay babies, if he could have found them at the time.

But watch out for liberals who get appointed police chief. It didn't take Hongisto long to show his true colors. As the saying goes, "Scratch a liberal and a fascist bleeds." This liberal bled a lot in a short time.

Hongisto was in office barely a month when the Rodney King decision was handed down in Simi Valley. Three white officers were acquitted of beating a black man who was down on the ground. The whole nation saw it replayed over and over in living color on their televisions. Hard to deny what happened. Except in lily white Simi Valley.

Naturally, people immediately took to the streets in San Francisco. An everyday occurrence in this city. Things got a little rowdy. (From what I've heard, things got a lot rowdier during the demonstrations against the Gulf War. I wasn't living here then, but the graffiti's still around.)

Faced with a night of justifiable anger spilling out into the streets of downtown San Francisco, Hongisto declared martial law. Well, he didn't call it that. He put a 9 PM curfew on the city, and suspended our right to assemble in the streets.

Martial law by any other name still means, "Step out of line and you're in the slammer, baby." And many people who were doing little more than exercising their right to free speech and to assemble in the streets found themselves in a cold jail cell. Welcome to Hongisto's America.

The newspapers went nuts, of course. San Francisco is not a city that tolerates martial law. The *San Francisco Bay Times*, a gay/lesbian/bisexual newspaper for which I write, ran a satirical cover with Hongisto's face pasted over a cop who's clutching a night stick at his groin. It looked as if the cop were jerking off with the night stick. The headline read: "Dick's Cool New Tool: Martial Law."

Guess what Hongisto did? From all accounts, he suggested that his officers get him a few ... thousand copies. He has a lot of relatives and friends, you see, who were just dying to see his photo on the cover of a queer newspaper.

It wasn't long before Hongisto was history, fired by the Police Commission after a round of hearings for allegedly ordering the newspapers stolen from their free vending boxes. Another liberal bites the dust after 45 days in office.

Again, I ask, if you can't trust the liberals, who can you trust? Yet we continue to support the Dianne Feinsteins and the Pete Wilsons and the Dick Hongistos because we say we have no other choice.

And most of the time we *don't* have any other choice. But we could put up more of a fight, make it more obvious that we're in a bind, not acquiesce so easily. As in the case of Hongisto. After he was fired as Police Commissioner, Hongisto tried for a seat on the San Francisco Board of Supervisors. He ran in a field of several contenders. There was no reason for anyone in the gay/lesbian/bisexual community to support him when there were others, including an out gay man, in the race.

Surprisingly, the *Bay Area Reporter*, another gay/lesbian newspaper in San Francisco, endorsed Hongisto in his bid for the Board of Supervisors, but not the two out queers who were also running. It is hard to understand how the *Bay Area Reporter* could support a man who violated the freedom of the press just because he was a longtime friend of the publisher.

Clinton—Unexpected Alternative to Bush

Enter Bill Clinton, former governor of Arkansas, shining white knight of the southern blonde variety, with a boy-next-door face. All-American as apple pie, at least to look at on the surface. Underneath: an extramarital affair, a lit joint, anti-war demonstrations.

Bill Clinton was the unexpected alternative to the man who had continued Ronald Reagan's genocidal policies on AIDS (insufficient funding, delays in treatment protocols and moral judgements disguised as public policy).

George Bush, the indifferent, watched while thousands died and countless others contracted a preventable disease. George Bush listened to the fundamentalists in his party like Pat Buchanan who saw AIDS as a retribution from their deity for the sodomites in godless places like San Francisco and New York.

George Bush exhibited no sympathy for people with AIDS (PWAs); his wife kissed a baby or two with AIDS and said a few kind words. At the height of the National Republican Convention's queerbashing, she had the gall to describe her party as "inclusive." She actually used that word.

To say that George and Barbara Bush were less than murderous in their treatment of AIDS and gays/lesbians/bisexuals in this country is to be accomplices in their crimes.

But who was this man called Clinton who surfaced from a nowhere state that hasn't been in the national spotlight since the early days of desegregation, a man who spoke of reforms that had not been uttered since the times of Jesse Jackson and his all-inclusive rainbow party?

Who, indeed?

Who is Clinton?

This is a man who claims to have always been a liberal, held back by the Neanderthal legislature in Little Rock from initiating progressive reforms in Arkansas, a man who had to throw caution to the wind in embracing queer folks. A man who was constantly torn between the right-wingers in his party who would have nothing to do with special interests, and those who wanted even more than Clinton the moderate could possibly endorse.

A man who went kicking and screaming into the long night of progressive ideas, terrified of abandoning the secure moderate road that America so admires of its politicians, a road that kept him in the governor's office for five terms.

This book looks at the man *The Nation* called "The Manufactured Candidate," and his relationship to the gay and lesbian community, a community that realized its fullest political influence during this last presidential election, a community that has been struggling for two decades to become part of that same electoral process.

A community that also knows—or should know—the dangers of working within a system that has yet to give justice to people of color, women, the aged, the poor, the disabled, the working class, the non-Anglos. A system that pours more money and resources into war than it ever has into feeding the starving or housing the poor.

A system that brags about its compassion while cutting welfare and turning away refugees from dictatorships it supports with dollars and guns.

A system that sends troops into Somalia to feed the starving with the same color faces as those who go hungry in the streets of America, yet hasn't sent the military to Harlem or Southeast Los Angeles to relieve the suffering.

A community torn, as much as Clinton himself, between Little Rock and a hard place.

1

Setting the Political Scene

FOR THE GAY/LESBIAN/BISEXUAL community, September 1992 was the worst of times. With the Democratic and Republican National Conventions out of the way, the community faced something it had never faced before: two statewide anti-gay/lesbian initiatives—one in Oregon, one in Colorado—as well as recall efforts against gay/lesbian rights legislation in Portland, Maine and Tampa, Florida.

The community also continued to be barraged with almost daily attacks from right-wing Republicans, such as presidential contender and columnist Pat Buchanan, who has never had a kind or reasonable thing to say about gays/lesbians/bisexuals or transgendered folks. In fact, the man has stirred up about as much hate and outright lies against gays/lesbians as Adolph Hitler did against the Jews.

The queer community woke up, almost daily, to hear tiresome double-talk gibberish from Republican President George Bush and Vice President Dan Quayle, gibberish that could be interpreted on the one hand as pro-gay/lesbian, and, on the other, as anti-queer.

Testing Grounds

The campaign for the anti-gay/lesbian initiative in Oregon was becoming particularly ugly, stirred up by the same kind of hate and lies as Buchanan regularly spread. Measure 9 would forbid the state from "condoning" homosexuality in any way, shape or form, as well as nix any gay/lesbian rights laws on the local or state level. By defining homosexuality as an abnormal lifestyle—akin to pedophilia (erotic attraction to children), sadism and masochism—the measure would affect schools, libraries, and social-service delivery.

In Colorado, Amendment 2 sought to repeal gay/lesbian rights laws in three cities—Aspen, Denver and Boulder—and prohibit the state or any of its cities or counties from passing similar measures.

Colorado, like Oregon and every other state in this nation, is a mix of the conservative and the liberal, the rural and the big city. In Colorado, Aspen, Boulder and Denver represent the more open-minded, live-and-let-live areas. In Oregon, the proverbial hotbeds of liberalism are centered around Portland and the college towns of Corvallis and Eugene.

It was apparent from the start that the resulting battles in these states would be close calls. They would also be litmus tests. The right would judge from the results of these latest assaults against the gay/lesbian community if the field would be ripe for such attempts throughout the country.

For the queer community, years of struggle could go down the drain overnight.

Not the First Time

This initiative type of legal attack had been tried before by the right-wing, but never on such a grand scale. In 1977, singer Anita Bryant, whose only real claim to fame was appearing in orange juice ads for the Florida Citrus Growers Association (and in being a second runner-up in the Miss America pageant), led a successful effort to repeal the Dade County, Florida gay/lesbian rights law.

That same year, a Republican state senator from Orange County, California, John Briggs, pushed a state-wide ballot initiative to keep gays and lesbians from teaching in the schools (Proposition 6, also known as the Briggs Initiative). It failed. But both initiatives left their trail of named and unnamed victims: murders, beatings, harassment. In some instances, homophobes attacking gays and lesbians made it quite clear that they were doing it as a supportive response to the efforts of Anita or Briggs.

It's not surprising. Whenever you unleash hate, violence is bound to follow. Yet right-wing leaders seldom, if ever, express any concern for the queerbashings that follow in the path of their hate-filled campaigns. Isn't it amazing that we never hear these same right-wingers come out against anti-gay/lesbian violence? They should stand on their pulpits, at their rallies, in their seminars and denounce it.

The Violence Builds

By the fall of 1992, several acts of vandalism had already been committed against the headquarters of gay/lesbian groups or the homes of activists connected with the No on 9 campaign in Oregon. Activists were seeing an increase in anti-gay/lesbian hate crimes, including the murder of a black lesbian and a white gay man. An older straight woman, part of an ecumenical group supporting gay/lesbian rights, had been accused of being a lesbian and had her life threatened.

The latter incident proved one thing: *anyone who worked against the amendment could be a target.* You didn't have to be gay or lesbian.

That's one of the things most non-gays don't realize about anti-gay/lesbian hate crimes: anyone can be perceived as queer, anyone can be harassed, anyone can be attacked. A few years ago a major network news program did a report on anti-gay/lesbian violence featuring a straight woman who had been attacked because she was thought to be a gay man.

It's not far-fetched.

In Wolf Creek, Oregon, Dean Decent told *Newsweek* (September 14, 1992) that violence against him and eight other out gay men was increasing. Decent said, "Now that the homophobes have blown up the car and shot at the trailer, when they drive by and yell it doesn't seem so bad."

The few months left until the November election were bound to get uglier. Many in the gay/lesbian/bisexual/transgendered community were terrified that more people were literally going to die for their rights before the election.

As for Colorado, the National Gay and Lesbian Task Force (NGLTF) and the Gay and Lesbian Community Center of Colorado reported an 87 percent rise in anti-queer violence, including a doubling of gay-related murders, following the introduction of Amendment 2.

Religious Industry Funded by Hate

A *Newsweek* article just two months before the election (September 14, 1992) postulated that the current right-wing attack against queers could be traced back to the 1989 Robert Mapplethorpe art retrospective that toured the country, stirring controversy at almost every stop because of its content.

That retrospective, funded in part by the National Endowment for the Arts (NEA) and including sexually explicit gay male photos (some with a sado-masochism theme) from the out queer photographer Mapplethorpe, aroused strong waves of protests from fundamentalists.

Why did the right jump on the Mapplethorpe bandwagon? *Newsweek* felt that the fall of the Berlin Wall in Germany and the Contras in Nicaragua had a lot to do with it. Without their usual commie scapegoats, the right needed something lucrative, a new guaranteed scapegoat, as a fundraising tool. A group that would make those viewers out in fundie TV land send in their ten- and twenty-dollar checks.

The fundamentalists (fundies for short) justify their fire-and-brimstone approach to homosexuality as Biblical orders from the man on high. The supreme one, they say, doesn't like queers. In fact, their deity wiped out two ancient cities of the plains—Sodom and Gomorrah—just to prove the point for all eternity.

Then there's the injunction in Leviticus that a man shouldn't lie with another man as he does with a woman. The destruction of Sodom and the passage from Leviticus are best-selling Biblical references in fundie circles. Fundamentalists use them to nix everything from hate crimes laws to domestic partners benefits for queers.

Vast amounts of money and influence are wielded by invoking these passages from the Bible. In the minds of the fundies and their faithful, nothing is worse than homosexuality—it destroys the very fabric of society.

Arguing the meaning of Biblical passages is futile at best. Biblical passages, especially those in the Old Testament, must be viewed in the context of another era, another culture, another language. In translation, words get misinterpreted, cultural mores are often viewed through one's own. The Bible has been translated more than once—from Hebrew to Latin to English.

Then, too, there is the issue of selectivity. The fundies ignore edicts they don't like—such as the one prohibiting the wearing of red or the eating of oysters—in favor of those which fill their coffers.

That's the key. An industry has grown around sin in this country, one that is intrinsic to most brands of Christianity (save the Quakers and the Unitarians). It's a fundamentalism so bent on saving souls that it often talks of creating a Christian America where no separation of church and state exists.

In the 1990's, queers are essential to solvency of this industry.

Hate Crimes Flourish

Hate crimes against gays/lesbians/bisexuals are one by-product of this industry. Not that every anti-gay/lesbian attack can be traced to the fundies. But the Bible-belters raise their share of hatred against the "queer menace." And they create an atmosphere in which hate against gays and lesbians can flourish.

A photo in *Newsweek* (September 14, 1992) says it all. "God Hates Fags" screams the sign held by the onlooker at the 1991 St. Patrick's Day Parade in Boston. A queer Irish contingent had to go to court in order to march in that parade.

The traditional Catholics in the Irish community were not pleased that gays and lesbians were wearing the green that day. In the New York St. Patrick's Day parade, Mayor David Dinkins marched with the Irish queers to show his solidarity. He was pelted with bottles.

If people feel, as the Irish onlookers did who carried anti-queer signs or who pelted Dinkins, that their deity hates "fags," then don't they have the divine seal of approval to act on that hate? Isn't killing queers doing God's work? Fundies say "love the sinner but hate the sin." Can people really keep that distinction clear?

History shows that people usually cannot. The hatred of the Jews in Europe led to the Nazi Holocaust. The hatred unleashed by Anita Bryant led to the bumper sticker and slogan, "Kill a Queer for Christ."

Hate crimes against gays and lesbians are business-as-usual throughout America every day of the week. They consist of murders, beatings and verbal harassment of persons believed to be gay, lesbian, bisexual or transgendered. Literally thousands of reported cases of these crimes exist in the records of organizations that keep track of them.

These thousands of cases are only the tip of the iceberg. Most gay/lesbian people do not report verbal harassment or even physical attacks. They're too scared of retribution from their attackers, or loss of family or jobs, should their sexual orientation become public.

NGLTF, which, among other things, tracks anti-gay/lesbian violence on the national level, released its latest findings on hate crime in March 1992. According to that report, which is issued annually, anti-gay/lesbian violence was up 31 percent in 1991. A total of 1,822 incidents were logged by NGLTF's Anti-Violence Project.

Those incidents come primarily from only five gay/
lesbian agencies keeping track of anti-gay/lesbian violence. If every anti-gay/lesbian incident that occurs in
this country were reported, the numbers would be stag-
gering. How many gay men and lesbians recall being
persecuted daily while growing up, verbally harassed
with names like "faggot" or "sissy" or "tomboy," even
beaten because we did not fit into society's rigid gender
roles? There wouldn't be enough paper to write up that
many reports. I'm not exaggerating.

In some states and cities, hate-crime laws which increase penalties for hate-motivated crimes include
sexual orientation as a protected category. In almost every instance, the inclusion of sexual orientation in these
bills is the most controversial aspect, invoking outrage
on the part of fundamentalists and cowardice on the
part of politicians.

Which is business-as-usual for any law that addresses the injustice done to queers.

The Republican Right Attacked
with Vengeance

Attacks by the Republican right against the queer community did not ease up during the entire year 1992. In
fact, they increased with an unparalleled venom and intensity—even when President George Bush and Vice
President Dan Quayle tried to soft peddle the anti-gay/
lesbian rhetoric, and even when they tried several times
to card themselves off (as ridiculous as this may sound)
as pro-gay/lesbian.

The right-wing feeding frenzy over gay/lesbian
rights issues became so intense that an innocuous state-

ment from Bush on having "no litmus test" for employment at the White House caused James A. Smith of the Southern Baptist Convention to lose his cool.

Smith said in no uncertain terms that the religious right could no longer deliver votes for the president until he "came clean" on the issue of gay/lesbian rights.

For the religious right, it seemed, Bush's stand on gay/lesbian rights was a litmus test. Bush had a real dilemma on his hands. If he came out too strongly against gay/lesbian rights, he alienated the moderates and the younger voters in his party. If he didn't bash queers, he stood a good chance of losing the fundamentalists who rode him into the White House in 1988.

His answer, and the party's: let all hell—and homophobia—break loose at the GOP convention. Damn the queers! Full speed ahead.

Highlights of Hate

Let's look at some highlights of the 1992 right-wing campaign to undermine the rising influence of the queer community in America.

Buchanan and the NEA

The year got off to a rousing start in February when Pat Buchanan, a presidential contender at the time, used excerpts from the Marlon Riggs' film, *Tongues Untied*, to attack his primary opponent George Bush. Buchanan made issue of the fact that the Bush administration's NEA funded *Tongues Untied*, a film that, in his words, "glorified homosexuality." (*Washington Post*, Feb. 27, 1992)

Riggs' film, which deals honestly and forcefully with

being black and gay in America, is a brilliant work of poetry and politics; it pulls no punches in condemning homophobia in the black community and racism in the gay/lesbian community.

Buchanan has never been concerned with either homophobia or racism. As a privileged straight white male, what does he know of these things? Educate himself? That's beneath him.

The Buchanan attack forced the hand of the Bush administration, which fired then-NEA chief, John Frohnmayer. Buchanan is one of the more virulent homophobes in politics—the kind of man who would have sold Jesus Christ to the Romans because he associated with a known prostitute.

Radice and the NEA

Ironically, Bush appointed Anne-Imelda Radice as the acting NEA chief, a right-wing woman widely reputed to be a lesbian. She did Bush's biding much better than Frohnmayer: she cut off funds from several gay/lesbian arts projects. Even arch conservative United States Senator Jesse Helms (a Republican from North Carolina), a man who relentlessly attacked queers on the Senate floor via speeches and legislation every chance he got, praised Radice.

Mosbacher Meeting with Gays/Lesbians

Buchanan came out swinging again that same month after Bush/Quayle campaign chair Robert Mosbacher met with representatives of the National Gay and Lesbian Task Force (NGLTF) and the AIDS Action Council. Mosbacher's daughter, Dee, who is an out lesbian, was instrumental in setting up the historic meeting.

Attending the session, which took place at Bush campaign headquarters in Washington, D.C., were Mosbacher, his assistant Diane Terpeluk, then-NGLTF head Urvashi Vaid, press spokesperson Robert Bray, NGLTF lobbyist Peri Jude Radecic and Jeff Levi, a former NGLTF head.

NGLTF requested four things of George Bush via Mosbacher: that he meet with queer leaders; that he appoint an out gay man or lesbian as liaison to his campaign; that he visit an AIDS service clinic; and that he include something about queers and adults with AIDS in future speeches. (If you followed their speeches and action, it was obvious that President and Mrs. Bush considered only AIDS babies safe enough to love.)

Mosbacher didn't give much indication that Bush would take the requests seriously, the *Washington Blade* reported. He did assure gay and lesbian leaders that he did not arrange the meeting "just to keep my daughter happy."

It didn't matter what Mosbacher said. Buchanan demanded, "I would like to see at least a statement from Mr. Bush that Mr. Mosbacher doesn't represent us, that he was off on a lark." (*Washington Times*, Feb. 21, 1992)

Buchanan was joined in his outrage by conservative congressional members and Morris Chapman, president of the Southern Baptist Convention. The cowards in the White House dismissed the meeting—via spokesperson Marlin Fitzwater—as "a matter of personal conscience because a daughter who is homosexual asked him to do it." (*Washington Post*, April 22, 1992)

Conservative Tea Party

Attempting to mend some fences, Bush held a little tea party in April for evangelical Christian activists at his taxpayer-supported residence. He told them that he opposed "special rights" for queers. He also expressed his disapproval of the District of Columbia's recently passed domestic partners bill, which extended health benefits to the same-sex lovers of city workers.

Republican Convention Platform Hearings

The following month, the Republican National Committee refused to allow three national queer groups— the National Gay and Lesbian Task Force (NGLTF), the Human Rights Campaign Fund (HRCF) and the National Federation of Log Cabin Clubs (gay/lesbian Republicans)—to testify at the Republican National Convention platform hearings.

This prompted gay Republicans to refuse to endorse the party's Bush and Quayle ticket. "I can't see that there's a lot of support [for Bush] right now, unless something very dramatic happens," said Richard Tafel, president of the National Federation of Log Cabins Clubs.

The Republican National Committee let queer organizations testify in 1988. But 1992 was different. An internal memo from Roy Jones, a campaign coalition aide, said, "Due to the administration's meetings with the gay political community, there is a growing fear that President Bush is going to endorse special privileges for the homosexual community."

Those meetings not only referred to the one between Mosbacher and NGLTF, but also to the administration's invitation to gay and lesbian leaders to attend two separate signings: for the Hate Crimes Statistics Act, which mandates the keeping of records on these crimes and includes sexual orientation as a category; and the Americans with Disabilities Act, a bill that extends rights to the disabled, including persons with AIDS.

Serious Threat to Children

In a May fundraising letter, Beverly LaHaye of Concerned Women of America and a regular at White House conservative brainstorming sessions, described the queer movement as "pos[ing] the most serious threat of all" to America's children.

Republican Party of Texas State Convention

In June, the Republican Party of Texas adopted a host of anti-gay/lesbian planks at its state convention in Dallas, among them support for the state's sodomy statute. Homosexuality is described in the platform as "a perversion of natural law ... biologically, morally and medically unsound."

Members of the Texas Log Cabin Club reported that they were harassed and threatened for passing out copies of their position paper on gay/lesbian rights. They say they were called "homos" and "faggots."

Republican National Committee
Platform Hearings

At the Republican National Committee platform hearings in Salt Lake City in June, NGLTF's Peri Jude Radecic managed to hand Utah Senator Orrin Hatch her organization's testimony, which included a demand for increased resources for AIDS, repeal of the ban on queers in the military, and passage of the federal gay/lesbian rights bill. She and other outsiders were not permitted into the hearings themselves, but relegated to an "overflow" room with heavy security.

Bush Campaign Worker Demoted

In July, Tyler Franz, an out gay man, charged the Bush campaign with discrimination, telling the D.C. Office of Human Rights that he was demoted to another job because he favored gay/lesbian rights in the GOP platform and opposed the party's gaybashing tactics.

Franz told ABC-TV's *Nightline*, "My belief is that the religious right was taking such a strong hold in the campaign that they were virtually taking over the campaign's direction."

HRCF Invitation Withdrawn

Also in July, an uproar arose after the Republican National Committee invited HRCF to a meeting to discuss plans for the upcoming convention and the election in general. Retorted Gary Bauer of the Family Research Council, "The Bush campaign better get its act together. You can't keep asking for and expecting traditional voters to support you when there are these constant efforts to play footsie with the gay rights movement."

The Republican Committee's response? The invitation was a mistake. But HRCF's spokesperson Gregory King had a different view. "The reason they invited us is because they know that … HRCF has made significant contributions to Republican candidates" who are pro-gay/lesbian.

Money talks, even if it's queer money.

Quayle, the Cultural Elite, and Murphy Brown

Vice President Quayle lost no time in joining the queer-bashing frenzy. In his June speech at the Southern Baptist Convention, Quayle said, referring to what he called the *cultural elite:* "They seem to think the family is an arbitrary arrangement of people who decide to live under the same roof, that fathers are dispensable and that parents need not be married or even of the opposite sexes. They are wrong." (*San Francisco Chronicle*, June 26, 1992)

The *San Francisco Bay Times* responded with a front-cover headline: "We Are the Cultural Elite and We Are Proud."

The cultural elite was a broad enough category to include the fictional TV character Murphy Brown, a non-lesbian news reporter who decides to become a single parent. Quayle's attack on Brown near the end of the spring 1992 season was good news for the producers of the show—the ratings for the first episode of the new fall season hit the roof.

Bush's Litmus Test

In a June interview Barbara Walters asked President Bush if he'd hire gay people. "We have no litmus test on that question here, and there aren't going to be any," Bush said. "And I would say, how do I know?"

He followed this quasi-queer support answer with a statement supporting the military's policy of barring queers from service. It was all part of an emerging pattern of double talk about queers from the folks in the White House. It's clear the GOP wanted the far-right vote on the one hand, and the gay Republican dollars on the other.

Quayle's Non-Discrimination Policy

A few weeks later, Quayle added coal to the fire by telling

CNN's Larry King that as far as employing gays and lesbians in the White House: "We have a policy of nondiscrimination." It was news to everyone.

Southern Baptist Convention's Smith was not pleased. "Quayle seems to state that the administration has a policy of homosexual protection that is not even required by law," he said, referring to the fact that federal law does not prohibit anti-gay/lesbian discrimination. "That's exactly the protection homosexuals are seeking in civil rights statutes." (*Washington Times*, July 24, 1992)

Bush and Quayle were in deep trouble now.

Said Smith, "Our problem with the Bush campaign and the White House is that they seem to be giving legitimacy to those who are seeking it. We oppose giving that legitimacy to homosexuals who demand special rights and privileges."

Added Smith, "We are not looking for a sexuality check at the door, but to say there is no litmus test is to say there is nothing an individual can do that would contradict our values. Would this president appoint a known pedophile?"

Smith cautioned the right-wing that though Clinton panders to queers, "… there is so much discontent with Bush that Clinton's guise as the moderate could make the difference."

False Television Ad

By October, the religious right became desperate and went for the gay/lesbian community's throat. In a 30-second television ad that was rejected by some stations as offensive, the Christian Action Network claimed that Clinton's vision includes "job quotas for homosexuals, giving homosexuals special civil rights, allowing homosexuals in the armed forces."

If only it were all true. Clinton never promised "job quotas" or "special" anything. The only true statement among the three is that Clinton supported lifting the ban on gays and lesbians in the military.

Not a Normal Lifestyle

In June, Bush told the *New York Times*, "I can't accept as normal lifestyle people of the same sex being parents. I'm very sorry. I don't accept that as normal. And I believe in the traditional values. And the best shot that a kid has is to have a mother and a father that love that child, that will educate that child, that will care for that child … and that's the best, and that can't happen for everybody. But to glamorize lifestyles that are, in my view, not the normal lifestyles, I don't approve of that. I don't want to censor it, but I don't approve of it."

That last sentence must have been the liberal part.

Asked for her opinion on the gay-isn't-normal line, quipped San Francisco Supervisor Roberta Achtenberg, who lives with her lover, California judge Mary Morgan, and their six-year-old son: "The feeling's mutual."

The White House take on Bush's remark? "He's just reiterating that he's a very traditional guy."

Bush: Love That Child

In August, just before the Republican Convention, Bush gave NBC's *Dateline* an interview in which he was asked what he would do if he had a gay or lesbian grandchild. His reply again displayed his use of double-talk around the gay/lesbian issue. Or, as the *Washington Blade* put it, demonstrated the tightrope he walked between "friends, [and] foes of Gays."

"I'd love that child," Bush said in his reply. "I would put my arm around him and I would hope that he wouldn't go out and try to convince people that this was the normal lifestyle—that this was an appropriate life-style, that this was the way it ought to be. But, I'd, I'd—you know, for me, I think the Bible teaches compassion and love. But I would say 'I hope you wouldn't become an advocate for a lifestyle that in my view is not normal and propose marriages of—same-sex marriages is a, is a normal way of life.' I don't … I'm not … I don't favor that."

Reporter Stone Phillips: "But would you be accept-ing?"

Bush: "But I would love that child."

Phillips repeated the question.

Bush: "Accepting in what sense?"

Phillips: "Accepting of the lifestyle that they would go on to lead?"

Bush: "Well, as I say, I would love that, I would love that person. And there's a difference between approving every step of the way and loving and treating with com-passion. And it's clear to me that the latter is what I'd want to do, and I wouldn't, I wouldn't—you know—condone necessarily of something that I felt, that I felt was, was not right."

It's clear Bush was not going to please either side.

Quayle and the Wrong Choice

Quayle did his own share of walking the tightrope on gay/lesbian issues later in the campaign. In an interview on ABC's *Primetime Live*, Quayle said he thought being gay was "a wrong choice that one makes." Yet he ap-proved of gay/lesbian teachers, "as long as they don't advocate their lifestyle as preferable." He also believed gays/lesbians should be able to live or work wherever they chose. "They do, and we have a policy of non-discrimination," he said. Again that mysterious nondiscrimination policy.

But the Quayle seal of approval did not extend to queer marriages. "I do not morally equate gay marriage with a heterosexual marriage," he said.

The Conventions: A Study in Contrast

As you will see in Chapter 2, nothing the right-wing could do during the first half of 1992 equalled the travesty that was to unfold at the Republican Convention, which was nothing short of a nightmare for queers. Quite a contrast from the Democrats, who one month before gave time for two people with AIDS and at least one openly lesbian politician to address the convention.

2

The Conventions

The Republican Convention

THE REPUBLICAN CONVENTION can best be described as gaybashing on a grander scale than ever seen in American politics, a charge out gay Republican John Schlafly, son of anti-feminist Phyllis, staunchly denies. But who can trust the word of a man dragged out of the closet? A man who doesn't believe queers can serve as good parents for a child because they're not partners of opposite sexes.

To set the proper tone, Buchanan started off the convention in a speech televised during prime time by agreeing with George Bush that he didn't believe "gay and lesbian couples should have the same standing in law as married men and women."

Attacking Clinton's agenda as pro-queer, pro-abortion and pro-women in the military, Buchanan said, "That's not the kind of change America needs. It is not the kind of change we can abide in a nation that we still call God's country." (*Washington Blade*, August 21, 1992)

Family Rights Forever

More gaybashing followed in the speeches given by Senator Don Nickles of Oklahoma and Pat Robertson of television's *700 Club*, a syndicated religious talk show with pitches for donations and frequent anti-gay attacks. Additionally, according to the *New York Times*, William Weld, who is the pro-gay/lesbian Governor of Massachusetts, was prevented from including pro-queer statements in his address by top officials of his party.

If the prevailing atmosphere of the convention wasn't obvious from the speeches, signs could be seen throughout the proceedings that read: "Family Rights Forever—Gay Rights Never."

Forget the economy, the GOP clearly wanted to keep all minds in America on one thing: the queer threat to the family. If that were eliminated, all would be well in America again. Unemployment lines would vanish, taxes would go down, the world would respect us again.

The Only Kind Words at the Convention

Mary Fisher, a woman with AIDS, managed to slip in the only kind words queers received that day. And, amazingly enough, she received applause for it. Just goes to show that there are some decent folks at a Republican Convention.

Said Fisher, "I ask you … to recognize that the AIDS virus is not a political creature. It does not care whether you are Democrat or Republican. It does not ask whether you are black or white, male or female, gay or straight, young or old."

Fisher continued, "Though I am female and contracted this disease in marriage and enjoy the warmth of my family, I am one with the lonely gay man sheltering a flickering candle from the cold winds of his family's rejection."

In a more admonishing note aimed at the fundamentalists in the audience, no doubt, Fisher said, "We have killed each other with our ignorance, our prejudice and our silence. We may take refuge in our stereotypes, but we cannot hide there long. Because HIV asks only one thing of those it attacks: 'Are you human?' And this is the right question—are you human?"

Actually, the inclusion of Fisher's speech was a brilliant strategy on the part of the GOP. How could they be accused of bashing queers when they allowed Fisher to speak? See, the Republicans aren't after queers. They just don't want the radical homosexual agenda being forced down America's throat. That's all.

The Media Didn't Buy It

It didn't sell. Even the major mainstream media such as *Time* magazine, the *New York Times*, and the *Washington Post* called the shenanigans at the convention what they were: queerbashing in the guise of defending "family values."

A *Time* headline (August 3, 1992) said it all by asking: "After Willie Horton Are Gays Next? Behind the GOP's 'family values' rhetoric lurks a plan to brand the Democrats soft on homosexuality." Willie Horton was the composite black convict used in racist Bush election campaign ads in 1988.

The *New York Times* decried the Republican platform, saying that it "goes out of its way to bash gay people." Indeed, the platform—"Our Vision Shared: Uniting Our Family, Our Country, Our World"—opposes gay rights legislation, upholds the Boy Scouts policy of excluding gay men, and rejects legislation legalizing gay/

lesbian marriages.

In the past decade, the right-wing and the religious right have used phrases like *family values* as cover-ups for their anti-gay/lesbian, anti-abortion agendas. Which prompted one San Francisco AIDS Foundation to adopt the phrase *family values* in connection with loving queer couples. They put out a poster that reads "Family Values" showing two men—one black, one white—embracing lovingly. It's a good strategy. Why let the right own those words? Queers have families, and family values, too.

Protesters Attacked

It is not surprising, given the tone of the speakers at the Republican Convention, that 2,000 peaceful protesters outside the convention center decrying the Bush record on AIDS were attacked by riot police on horseback and on foot. At least three people wound up in the hospital, with dozens more injured. Six people were arrested.

Protesters claimed that the police never issued a dispersal order before they charged into the crowd. Police, of course, said that they did. Suzanne Donovan, executive director of the American Civil Liberties Union of Texas, told the *Washington Blade* that her ten observers at the demonstration concluded that "the police very much over-reacted."

Police over-reaction to demonstrations is a fine tradition in America. Who can forget such shining moments as police attacking civil rights marchers in the 60's and gassing the crowds outside the Democratic Convention in Chicago in 1968? But AIDS activists are used to police tactics. Undaunted, activists disrupted speeches by George Bush and the Rev. Jerry Falwell (of Moral Majority fame) at separate functions during the convention.

Mrs. Bush and the Inclusive Party

In keeping with the unpredictable double-talk of the Bush White House on the issue of queers, Barbara Bush told PBS reporter Judy Woodruff during the convention that the Republican Party is inclusive. The response came to a question about whether gays were welcomed in the party.

"We're an inclusive party," said Mrs. Bush. "And I don't judge people, and I'm not fighting with them either. I'm telling you—you asked me what I think."

Despite what Mrs. Bush said, the message at the convention was clearly one of exclusion. Not only were queers unwelcome in the Republican Party that met in Texas in August 1992, the GOP vowed to fight any attempt queers made to gain any entry into the society at large via rights legislation and presidential executive orders.

Believe it or not, some gays and lesbians clung to the Republican Party despite its convention rampage against our rights. In the midst of the bashing, Marvin Liebman told the *Los Angeles Times* on August 20, "To be gay, conservative and Republican is not a contradiction." Liebman, a longtime conservative activist, founder of the Young Americans for Freedom and of the American Conservative Union, continued, "I'm proud to be all three, less proud this week to be a Republican."

While it's important for queers to be everywhere, including the Republican Convention, sometimes I don't understand how anyone can stand to be in the center of that much hatred.

Incidentally, members of the National Federation of Log Cabin Clubs did not endorse the Bush/Quayle ticket. For obvious reasons.

Bush Campaign Tries an About-face

After the convention, when it was obvious that the scapegoating of queers wasn't going to work, the Bush campaign tried an about-face. In September, while being interviewed on a Los Angeles TV talk show, Quayle said that "we are the ones that have implemented a non-discrimination policy when it comes to gays and lesbians. That is the administration's record, and we are proud of that record."

The comment came in response to a call-in viewer who said that speakers at the GOP convention "attacked and degraded" queers.

"Listen to what the president says and what I say," said the vice president. "I don't think you heard any of that rhetoric coming from me. You didn't hear it from the president."

This is the same vice president who said in his speech at the convention that the gay lifestyle is "wrong." And who said, after the convention, that being gay is "a wrong choice."

Gay/lesbian rights leaders in the District of Columbia had never heard of a non-discrimination policy from the White House. NGLTF's Bray said that Quayle was "shamelessly" trying to steer away from the queerbashing of the GOP convention. "Their own polls tell them the tactic has backfired," he said.

Center Stage with the Democrats

In sharp contrast to the Republican Convention, gay/lesbian rights and compassion for people with AIDS took center stage at the Democratic Convention for the first time in the 20 years that queers had been working within the Democratic Party.

The history of that involvement began when activists Jim Foster (now deceased) and Madeline Davis addressed the 1972 convention in Miami. Their speeches were not scheduled during prime time, however.

Mel Boozer, a black gay man, addressed the 1980 Democratic Convention for a whole ten minutes: "I know what it means to be called a nigger," he said. "I know what it means to be called a faggot. And I can sum up the difference in one word: none."

Boozer, who has since died of AIDS, offered himself up as a vice presidential candidate, then withdrew in favor of Walter Mondale. But not before he made history. "I think we really woke people up," activist Tom Bastow said of the speech. "It was the first time these people heard what we were saying." (*QW*, July 19, 1992)

The result? The party agreed to add sexual orientation to its list of anti-discrimination planks.

The 1992 Key Players

Fast forward to the 1992 Democratic primary. The key players, most of whom were out of the race by the convention, were: Former Senator Paul Tsongas of Massachusetts; Senator Bob Kerrey of Nebraska; Senator Tom Harkin of Iowa; and former California Governor Jerry Brown.

Tsongas had the best gay rights record, having introduced federal gay/lesbian rights legislation in 1979; he also aided in getting the 1980 gay rights plank into the Democratic platform. It was a great disappointment to many progressives in the gay/lesbian community when he announced in March that he was dropping out of the race due to a lack of funds.

Kerrey was problematic: as a member of the Lincoln,

Nebraska Human Rights Commission, he voted for a gay rights ordinance; yet he refused to sponsor the federal gay/lesbian rights bill. He once described homosexuality as "morally wrong."

Harkin also has a troubling record on gay/lesbian issues. When pressed by reporters as to why he would not support the federal gay rights bill, Harkin said, "Do you want to just feel good about yourself or win and then make a change?"

Jerry Brown, affectionately known as "Governor Moonbeam," was good on gay/lesbian issues while chief executive of California, but he was a longshot in the primary. As governor, Brown issued an executive order banning anti-gay/lesbian discrimination in state government, came out against the Briggs Initiative, signed the state's sodomy repeal law, made several appointments of out queers, and issued gay/lesbian pride day proclamations.

The most likely choice for queers was Tsongas, but as time went on, Bill Clinton, the party favorite, seemed to be shaping up as a pro-gay/lesbian candidate, despite the initial reservations about him from the ACT UP front.

ACT UP

ACT UP is the AIDS Coalition To Unleash Power, the radical AIDS activist group that has, more than any other group, made AIDS activism a household word. More often than not, ACT UP is the bad cop of the AIDS activist front, screaming the loudest and compromising the least.

Everybody from former president George Bush on down, it seems, has condemned ACT UP at one time or another for its rude tactics. But rude is what ACT UP strives for.

It was ACT UP that organized the controversial demonstration at St. Patrick's Cathedral in New York City a few years ago. During that protest of Cardinal John Cook's stance against condoms, activists disrupted mass; one demonstrator, pretending to be a devotee, went to the altar for Holy Communion and when offered the wafer, tossed it on the floor.

The uproar over that "desecration of the host" went on for weeks. Many in the queer community were quick to condemn ACT UP for this action. But those folks lost sight of the fact that nothing activists could do short of murder equals what the church has done by opposing sound public health policy, such as the distribution of condoms and the teaching of safe sex. An institution such as the Roman Catholic Church wields a lot of influence. Imagine what would happen if the church endorsed condom use and the teaching of life-saving safe sex practices.

Critics of ACT UP also lose sight of the fact that this group has successfully pushed the Federal Drug Administration to move on new AIDS drugs and protocols. Without ACT UP, the fight against AIDS would be no further than it was ten years ago.

ACT UP had serious reservations about Bill Clinton; basically, they focused on his poor record on gay/lesbian rights and AIDS while he was governor of Arkansas.

An Influential Factor in Electoral Process

Despite whatever reservations ACT UP or anyone else had about Bill Clinton, there's no doubt that the 1992 Democratic National Convention marked the emergence of queers as an influential factor in the electoral process in this country. This historic new age could prove just as scary as it is exciting for queers. *Scary* because of what it could mean for the future of the gay/lesbian movement in America, a topic I will return to in a later chapter. *Exciting* because out-front queers and queer issues were, for the first time, an essential part of the convention. The gay/lesbian caucus at the convention—108 members strong, a record number—was wooed by everyone from Diane Feinstein to New York Mayor David Dinkins ("You matter a great deal," he said) to Bill Clinton (who sent his greetings).

Out queer Massachusetts United States Representative Barney Frank told the delegates to forget their reservations about the man from Little Rock because of his record on AIDS and sodomy. "You can criticize him the day he takes office," he said. "But you'll be much better off having to criticize *him*."

Two speakers with AIDS addressed the convention: Bob Hattoy, a gay man and a friend of Clinton's, and Elizabeth Glaser, wife of Paul Michael Glaser (of television's *Starsky and Hutch*). At the time of his diagnosis, Hattoy was environmental policy advisor to Clinton; Glaser was infected through a blood transfusion and passed it on to her two children. One of them is now dead.

While their presentations were dramatic and powerful, there was one question on many minds: do they represent the myriad faces of AIDS in America? Neither is a person of color; neither is poor; neither has a problem accessing health care in a country that has no national plan to cover its citizens.

The Face of AIDS

In terms of exposing America to the *fact* of AIDS, their speeches made a world of difference. But at least one of those faces should have belonged to a person of color.

As Thomas B. Stoddard, a gay rights leader in New York City, told the *New York Times* (July 14, 1992), "She's a celebrity and he's a campaign worker. It's a false image of AIDS. It's a mistake not to have a person of color." He goes on to say, "The true nature of HIV is the lack of basic health care that tens of thousands of individuals must confront by nature of poverty and other conditions."

The queer community is not monolithic. It is composed of people of all races, ethnic backgrounds, socioeconomic levels, classes, degrees of openness, and so forth. The "gay agenda" that you read about in the newspapers does not represent every segment of the gay community. The "gay agenda" is, in fact, many agendas. Stoddard's comments raise an important question for the queer community: which agenda should we pursue?

Consider this: what does a federal gay/lesbian rights bill mean to a poor black drag queen (transvestite) who survives by working the streets of New York City? Will this person's life be any easier because Congress decides that she has the right to a job as a gay person?

Congress decided she had rights as a black person 30 years ago. And what has that done for her? She still can't put food on the table without giving blowjobs on 42nd Street.

The decision by Democratic Convention organizers not to include a person of color with AIDS brings that issue home. How can any group represent AIDS in 1992 without acknowledging the tremendous toll it has taken, and continues to take, in communities of color?

Surely, someone in the queer community must have been in a position to say to Bill Clinton, "Hey, one of these speakers should be black or Latino or Native American or Asian. One of these speakers must represent the new face of AIDS."

A Gay Man With AIDS

Hattoy and Glaser's speeches were powerful, especially to those in middle America who may never have heard a real person with AIDS (that is, not an actor on a TV show) speak. For the delegates in the room, straight and queer alike, it was difficult to keep a dry eye.

"I am a gay man with AIDS," Hattoy said, as quoted in the *Washington Blade* (July 17, 1992). "If there is any honor in having this disease, it's the honor of being part of the gay and lesbian community in America.

"We have watched our friends and lovers die, but we have not given up. Gay men and lesbians created community health clinics, provided educational materials, opened food kitchens, and held the hands of the dying in hospices. The gay and lesbian community is a family in the best sense of the word."

Later he said, "We need a president who will take action. A president strong enough to take on the insurance companies that drop people with the AIDS virus. A president courageous enough to take on the drug companies that drop people with the HIV virus. A president who is not terrified of the word 'condom.'

"We're part of the American family, Mr. President. Your family has AIDS," he said. "We're dying, and you are doing nothing about it. Listen, I don't want to die. But I don't want to live in an America where the president sees me as the enemy.

"We are the doctors and lawyers, folks in the military, ministers, rabbis and priests. We are Democrats. And yes, Mr. President, Republicans. We're part of the American family."

Glaser, too, attacked Bush and his administration. "When anyone tells President Bush that the battle against AIDS is seriously under funded, he juggles the numbers to mislead the public into thinking we're spending twice as much as we really are," she said.

The Party Platform

San Francisco Supervisor Roberta Achtenberg also addressed the 1992 Democratic Convention. An early supporter of Clinton, she sat on the National Democratic Platform Drafting Committee, and helped forge a pro-gay/lesbian, pro-woman document.

"The Democratic Platform is the party's cornerstone policy document for the next four years, and an essential component of the plan to be pursued by a Bill Clinton administration," she said just prior to the convention. In her convention speech, Achtenberg described the platform as "a plan for rebuilding our economy and rededicating ourselves to social justice."

In the area of **civil rights**, the platform directs party leadership to support: the fight against discrimination on any basis, including race, gender, national origin, religion, age, disability, and sexual orientation; employment and civil rights protection for gay men and lesbians; voting rights, including language access to voting ratification of the ERA; equitable remedies and pay equity for women; aggressive prosecution of hate crimes; full enforcement of the Americans with Disabilities Act; the honoring of treaty commitments with Native Americans; and an end to military discrimination against queers.

In the area of AIDS, the platform includes: implementation of the recommendations of the National Commission on AIDS; access to quality care for everyone with HIV; and speed-up of the FDA drug approval process.

In terms of **women's health**, the platform redirects federal research priorities to breast, cervical and ovarian cancer as well as reproductive health and infertility.

Achtenberg's appointment to the Platform Committee was not tokenism: four other gay men and lesbians served on its Credential and Rules Committees.

Achtenberg said, "All of us who have lived through this year of distrust and dashed dreams yearn for the day when America will be a just society, with real opportunity for all. With the adoption of this platform, the election of Bill Clinton, the ceaseless work of all our people, we can bring that day closer. I can hardly wait."

Clinton Selected as Candidate

Then came the big moment: Bill Clinton's selection as the Democratic candidate. Clinton didn't forget gays and lesbians in his acceptance speech. "We need each other," he said. "All of us. … We don't have a person to waste. … And yet for too long politicians have told the most of us that are doing all right that what's really wrong with America is the rest of us. Them. Them the minorities … them the liberals. Them the poor. Them the gays. We've gotten to where we've nearly them-ed ourselves to death. Them and them and them. But this is America. There is no them; there is only us."

We need to bear in mind, however, that Clinton's mention of AIDS in his acceptance speech was a last-minute addition, according to the *New Republic* (January 4 & 11, 1992 issue). "Clinton mentioned AIDS … only after gay supporters who obtained a leaked copy lobbied furiously for the penciled-in change."

The Smell of Victory

It was clear from the speeches at the convention, many of which mentioned queers, and the warm reception gay/lesbian activists and delegates received that the times were indeed changing.

In fact, these developments were probably more monumental than anything Bill Clinton said in his acceptance speech. Queers were an integral part of the process and the workings of that convention. Some of that was due to Bill Clinton. The rest was due to a lot of hard work on the part of activists.

For the queer community in the fall of 1992, the smell of victory was already in the air: a party that once rejected gays/lesbians had been seduced and conquered. As Robert Bray, NGLTF spokesperson, said, "Back in 1988, not even the Democrats returned our calls. Now we find ourselves at the highest level of political power, with tremendous access. It's an enormously seductive and exciting atmosphere."

But that's not how it began. For Bill Clinton, the early days of the campaign trail were anything but quiet. Bill Clinton was a hunted man, pursued not only by his record as governor of Arkansas, but, more importantly, by a handful of ACT UP members determined to demand accountability for that record from the man they called "Slick Willie."

Calling themselves the Presidential Project, those ACT UP members managed to confront Clinton at many stops on the early campaign trail. It was as if they were an avenging spirit, springing from the air, refusing to be silenced, no matter what Clinton said or did.

3

Clinton Then and Now

ARKANSAS WOULD HARDLY have inspired Cole Porter to write "Anything Goes." In fact, little goes in the Southern state except farming and wholesome looks. For queers, Arkansas may as well be Siberia; Little Rock, the state capital, is the only haven, with a handful of queer bars.

During the primary race, queer activists in Arkansas asked those outside the rural state to examine five-term governor Bill Clinton's record on AIDS and sodomy reform in light of a legislature that may very well consider Pat Buchanan a liberal.

These activists said that "the Clinton man" did the best he could. They pointed to his liberal state Health Department as proof of his sincerity in wanting good public health policy that was not based on ignorance or fear.

Still, there were those outside Arkansas who said he could have done more to help the fight against AIDS in Arkansas. Others agreed, adding that if he couldn't do it in Arkansas, how was he going to do it with a whole country to battle, a country that had many states like Arkansas, and many legislators like those in Little Rock?

AIDSphobic Legislation Under Clinton's Administration

A look at Governor Bill Clinton's record on AIDS in Arkansas reveals that in addition to failing to fight for adequate state AIDS funding, he signed three pieces of legislation that AIDS activists—particularly those in the ACT UP Presidential Project—found objectionable or AIDSphobic, as they say:

- Mandatory HIV testing.
- Criminalization of the transmission of HIV.
- Reporting of the names of HIV-positive individuals.

Mandatory Testing

The idea of mandatory testing sounds alarms in the hearts of most AIDS activists. And for good reason. Given the stigmatizing and often traumatizing nature of AIDS, one cannot take lightly the decision to be tested.

One can lose a job, housing, even one's life if HIV-positive status is known. Houses have been torched because a child inside was HIV-positive or had AIDS. In America. In Florida. That's why city and state legislatures have passed laws to outlaw discrimination based on HIV status or AIDS diagnosis. That's why strict confidentiality laws exist in many of these same localities.

For the record, Dr. Joycelyn Elders, the Clinton-appointed head of the Arkansas Health Department (and now his choice for United States Surgeon General), and her staff opposed the original testing bill, which included 18-to-20 scenarios under which someone could be forced to face his or her HIV status.

Elders, 59, a pediatrician, was a liberal in a state where such a label was anathema to getting things done. Still, Elders and Clinton's other public health people managed to negotiate with a Neanderthal legislature and obtain the present bill, which calls for the testing of only health-care workers stuck with a needle, persons charged with sexual offenses, and patients who need it as part of their treatment.

Criminalization of Transmission Bill

The criminalization of transmission bill—which condemns a person who knowingly transmits HIV to six-to-thirty years in prison and/or a $15,000 fine—went through the same sort of negotiating to water it down. In its final form, it exempts from prosecution persons who disclose their HIV status.

The Reporting Bill

The reporting bill, which requires the names of all persons testing positive to be reported to the Arkansas Health Department, invokes nightmares for AIDS activists. Having names on file—even under the tightest security—is no guarantee that they will not get out. Any system can be breached or compromised. And, as I said before, disclosure of one's HIV status can have devastating effects.

Of course results are to be kept confidential. But what comfort is this in a state that provides no teeth to its confidentiality laws, that is, no criminal or civil penalties for disclosing this information?

Clinton couldn't get out of this one: Elders and the Health Department supported the reporting of names. Why? In a written explanation to the Human Rights

Campaign Fund in Washington, a leading gay activist in Arkansas stated, "It was thought necessary to public health in a rural state such as Arkansas to have accurate statistics to know where the infection was going, as opposed to where the disease was." The activist also noted, "The Health Department is the governor."

In the 1991 regular session of the Arkansas legislature, 18 AIDsphobic bills were drafted, but none of these was introduced due to the intervention of the Clinton Health Department.

It seemed like Clinton was doing something on AIDS, that is, responding to repressive legislation as it came along, trying to keep the wolves in the legislature at bay. His other legislative failures, however, are not as easily explained or excused. For example, activists rightly point to the fact that only federal money was spent in fighting AIDS in Arkansas until 1991. Ten years into the epidemic.

Sodomy Reform

Clinton's record on sodomy reform was another serious thorn in his (and our) side. In 1977–78, when Clinton was state attorney general, the legislature reinstated sodomy in Arkansas' revised criminal code, making it gay-specific. In other words, no mention was made of heterosexual sodomy, which was eliminated as a criminal offense in the new code.

A class A misdemeanor, sodomy is defined in the Arkansas code as "any act of sexual gratification involving: 1) the penetration, however slight, of the anus or mouth of an animal or a person by the penis of a person of the same sex or an animal; or 2) the penetration, however slight, of the vagina or anus of an animal or a person by any body member of the same sex or an animal."

Quipped Wayne Turner and Steve Michael of the ACT UP Presidential Project in a press release in March 1992: "This law places same-sex loving relationships in the same category as a farmer in Pine Bluff, Arkansas slamming his cock in the poop chute of one of those scrawny Arkansas chickens that Washington State and California Chicken Farmer Associations warn us about."

Many saw Attorney General Bill Clinton as helpless against the conservative and determined legislative regime; others saw him as an uncaring villain.

Why didn't Bill Clinton speak up against the sodomy law in Arkansas? Queers had to wait 15 years for Clinton's answer—and it is suspect at best.

"Nobody asked me about it," is what Clinton said, under pressure from queer activists during the election campaign. "When it passed 15 years ago—when I was attorney general—I did what I could to defeat it. I thought it was in error. There was no public statement. I just lobbied against it." And later in the same interview Clinton said, "There is no point in talking about it, but I didn't like it."

An attempt to kill the sodomy law failed in 1991. The sponsor of that effort, Senator Vic Snyder, said, "The obstacle was not Bill Clinton or anyone in the governor's office. The obstacle was the legislature."

According to the *Philadelphia Gay News* (June 6–12, 1992), Betsy Wright, Clinton's former chief of state, said that the governor of Arkansas didn't know the sodomy repeal had been introduced. Why? Because he was occupied with his own legislative agenda. Which obviously didn't include queers.

It's true that queers in Arkansas had been lax in asking politicians, including Governor Clinton, the kinds of questions they're routinely asked in big cities across

America. They should have nailed him about the sodomy law in the late 70's when it was reinstated. They should have been on his case once he became governor. They certainly should have been after him once Snyder introduced the 1991 repeal bill.

If Bill Clinton really believed the sodomy law was so wrong, wouldn't someone have known? As John R. Starr, managing editor of the *Arkansas Democrat-Gazette*, wrote of Clinton's lobbying claims (May 27, 1992), "If so, he made sure he didn't get caught doing it." Starr concluded, "If Clinton loses the presidential race... and he doesn't have the character and the courage to introduce his own repealer in 1993, he should at least fulfill his campaign promise to the homosexual community by supporting Snyder's."

Columnist Paul Greenberg in the *Arkansas Democrat-Gazette* (May 24, 1992) expressed even greater cynicism about Bill Clinton. "The governor can rightly claim that he's done everything to secure homosexual rights that was politically safe."

In the same column Greenberg wrote, "Who says [Clinton] has no stand on civil rights for homosexuals? He's got at least two—one for New York and one for Arkansas, one as governor and one as presidential candidate."

Greenberg squarely hammered that nail. It easy for Bill Clinton to say he lobbied against the sodomy law behind the scenes; how can it be verified? It could also be a convenient political answer for a case of cowardice or neglect.

And if Clinton were so pro-queer, why did he refuse to issue a Coming Out Day proclamation in 1989? The official explanation was that it didn't affect enough people. Surely many of Arkansas' other proclamations affect as small a population as Coming Out Day.

Clinton's AIDS Platform

His record on AIDS and sodomy was problematic for Bill Clinton as he traveled around the country, intent on winning the queer vote. Especially with those tireless ACT UP radicals on his trail like a pack of wolves, constantly reminding him of things he wanted buried. They were out for blood. What could Clinton do?

There was only one solution. Concoct an AIDS platform.

In a session arranged by longtime friend and gay activist David Mixner, Bill Clinton met with AIDS activists in April 1992. Following that meeting, an AIDS position was formulated.

The course was set. Bill Clinton was on his way to becoming the darling of the gay set.

4

Gay Activists and the Clinton Campaign

FOR THE MEMBERS of the ACT UP Presidential Project, Bill Clinton was not the ideal candidate to oppose the murderous George Bush. In fact, they believed Clinton had forsaken the queer community in Little Rock and would do it again if he got into the White House.

Genesis of the ACT UP Presidential Project

February 1992: Downtown Manchester, New Hampshire, a few days before the first presidential primary. Over a thousand people take to the streets to raise the AIDS issue, to make their stand that little has been done to fight this disease. For almost two hours, activists blocked Elm Street, according to a report in Boston's *Bay Windows*. Though they don't manage to disrupt any of the campaign speeches, they do disrupt Bush's address at a high school.

This is the birthplace of the raucous Presidential Project. Its five-month mission: to force the candidates in the primary, both Democratic and Republican, to address AIDS and gay/lesbian rights. In fact, these ACT UP folks wanted AIDS to be a leading issue in the race.

For the next few months, Presidential Project members, particularly Steve Michael and Wayne Turner, dogged Clinton about his stand on AIDS. They attacked other candidates, too, but as it became clear that Clinton was the man for the non-Bush crowd, they intensified their badgering of the governor from Arkansas.

When all is said and done, Clinton has the distinction of being the candidate most badgered by queer activists during any recent presidential campaign, an honor I'm sure he is not writing home about.

What did these activists want from Clinton? A release from the ACT UP folks on March 19, 1992 asked that Governor Clinton call a special session of the Arkansas legislature to, among other things: repeal the sodomy law, repeal the objectionable AIDS laws, and implement a statewide HIV/AIDS education and prevention program based on the recommendations of the National Commission on AIDS.

Not ones to mince words, the ACT UP members wrote, "Clinton's shameful record of inaction and indifference on AIDS makes him personally responsible for every HIV infection and death in the state of Arkansas. Slick Willie has blood on his hands."

Presidential Project Persistence

One shining example of the persistence of the ACT UP Presidential Project was seen in Connecticut at the end of March 1992. Joined by New England ACT UP members, the Presidential Project folks were welcomed by Clinton at a gathering in the Bridgeport Community Center. Clinton used the opportunity to trash the Bush administration's policy on AIDS.

Then Frank Smithson of the Presidential Project took the microphone. After denouncing some of the Arkansas AIDS laws that Clinton signed, Smithson said, "I want you to talk about AIDS every day. Not just when you see an ACT UP tee-shirt or sign, mind you, but every day. Understand?"

At a Marshall's department store in New Haven, Smithson again confronted Clinton. "Bill, Bill," shouted the AIDS activist. "Have you talked about AIDS today? You better have talked about AIDS today." When Clinton assured the activist that he talked about the disease at a high school that day, Smithson replied, "You've been ignoring AIDS in Arkansas, Bill. We're not going to let you ignore it here."

And they didn't. Activists continued nagging Bill Clinton. Perhaps the most widely publicized confrontation came at a gathering of lawyers at the Laura Belle Club in New York City at the end of March. It drew a more volatile response from Bill Clinton. The *New York Daily News'* headline screamed, in huge print, "Boiling Bill blasts back." The accompanying photo showed an open-mouthed Clinton almost face to face with an equally angry Bob Rafsky of ACT UP/New York.

The following is an excerpt from a transcript of that confrontation published in the *New York Times.*

Rafsky: "[New York] is the center of the AIDS epidemic, what are you going to do about AIDS? Are you going to start a war on AIDS? Are you going to put somebody in charge? Are you going to do more than you did while you were governor of Arkansas? We're dying in this state. What are you going to do about AIDS?"

Clinton: "Can we talk now?" Rafsky gave Clinton the go-ahead to talk. "Most places where I go, nobody wants to talk. They want us to listen to them. I'm listening. You can talk. I know how it hurts. I've got friends who've died of AIDS."

Rafsky: "Bill, we're not dying of AIDS as much as we are from 11 years of government neglect."

Clinton: "And that's why I'm running for president, to do something about it. I'll tell you what I'll do. I'll tell you what I'd do. First of all I would not just talk about it in campaign speeches; it would become a part of my obsession as president. There are two AIDS Commission reports gathering dust somewhere in the White House, presented by a commission appointed by a Republican president. There's some good recommendations in there. I would implement the recommendations of the AIDS Commission. I would broaden the HIV definition to include women and IV drug users, for more research and development and treatment purposes."

Rafsky kept up the attack, accusing Clinton of "dying of ambition." Clinton got defensive at this point, taking the attack personally.

Clinton: "You do not have the right to treat human beings, including me, with disrespect because of what you're worried about. I did not cause it. I am trying to do something about it. I have treated you and all the people who interrupted my rally with a hell of a lot more respect than you've treated me, and it's time you started thinking about that."

Clinton went on for a long time, obviously angry at Rafsky's persistence. He concluded by saying, "There are other choices on the ballot. Go get them is my answer to you. If you want somebody that'll fight AIDS, vote for me because when I come in to do something, I do it, and I fight for it."

ACT UP made Clinton lose his cool again in Sunrise, Florida. He told activists needling him, "I'm through with you, I'm through with all of you."

More Than a Disease

This kind of badgering was not unusual for the AIDS activists from around the country who felt uneasy about a man with Clinton's record. They kept the pressure at an intense level for weeks.

For the queer community, AIDS is more than a disease, more than a cause. It's a symbol, a real living breathing concrete symbol of how murderous America can be.

The history of AIDS is more than one of neglect, ignorance and homophobia. It is the story of thousands of gay men dying without the dignity afforded those with other illnesses; gay men stigmatized because AIDS is sexually transmitted and because the disease first struck them; gay men made to feel that they deserve exactly what they got.

It is the story of a health care system ruled by bigotry that treated the early cases of AIDS as if they were the bubonic plague come back to life; as if the gay men who contracted it were an inconvenience at best, a bunch of careless promiscuous men who endangered the blood supply and put millions of decent normal folks at risk.

It is the story of a service delivery system that should be without moral judgement but that was often no better in the first years of AIDS than the fundamentalists in their ivory tower pulpits.

In those first few years of the epidemic, queers heard countless tales of food being left out of reach, of doctors afraid to treat someone who was gay, of insurance companies that would not cover certain zip codes, like the Castro's 94114, because of the risk of AIDS.

Reagan Administration: Policy of Genocide

Ronald Reagan was president when AIDS first hit the headlines in 1981. His administration's policy for the first few years is described as genocidal by many in the AIDS activist movement. Let the queers die. Virtually no federal money was allocated against the disease in those first years.

Compare that dismal fact with what happened when Legionnaire's Disease hit a small group of conventioneers at a posh hotel in Philadelphia—white businessmen every one of them. As could be expected, every resource was put at the disposal of health officials to find the cause for this illness. With enough money and resources, it didn't take long to find the microscopic culprit in the air conditioning ducts.

The System Doesn't Work

For six or seven years, the gay community tried its best to tread lightly but still lobby for more funds, more research. But it wasn't until ACT UP emerged on the scene that things began to change for the better. By then, thousands and thousands of gay men were dead. Still, even with ACT UP the changes were small and slow to be enacted. Especially with the Bush administration. It was a frustrating time.

At the start of the primary, 137,000 Americans had died of AIDS, a good portion of them gay or bisexual. No wonder ACT UP's tactics were so loud and rude during the primary. Gay men don't expect the system to work for them. Gay men don't expect that politicians really care about their health, their future, their lives. Gay men don't expect support from churches, the medical establishment, the laws.

It's no surprise that Bill Clinton received the same treatment as any other politician. It's no wonder his record in Arkansas was looked upon as absolute proof that he couldn't be trusted, no matter what he said to the contrary, no matter how much explaining he did, no matter what promises he made for a brighter future.

As far as the ACT UP activists were concerned, Bill Clinton was part of an establishment that had left many of their friends to die. Far too many in the gay community can point to at least a dozen friends who are dead from AIDS; some, like ACT UP founder and playwright Larry Kramer, can even name a hundred or more folks they've known who've succumbed to the disease.

Queer Nation Joins In

ACT UP wasn't the only group from the gay/lesbian community confronting Bill Clinton. Another radical action group, Queer Nation, which believes in loud and rude behavior on gay/lesbian issues, demonstrated against him during a splashy "Broadway for Bill" fundraiser in New York City on June 22, 1992.

Disrupting the benefit ("Gays Crash Bill Bash," the *New York Daily News* headline read), which featured Alec Baldwin, Richard Dreyfuss and Blair Brown, demonstrators wanted to know about the reinstatement of the Arkansas sodomy law when Clinton was attorney general.

Clinton said, "That's right. I was attorney general. I wasn't governor. I didn't sign the law. I did my best to defeat the law. Those are the facts." When the heckling would not stop, the demonstrators were evicted.

The tireless efforts of the ACT UP Presidential Project did score some victories. In May, Project members Michael Petrelis and Carl Goodman got Clinton to speak out publicly against the sodomy law in his home state.

No Other Choice

The ACT UP Presidential Project and Queer Nation did not represent the entire queer movement in America. More mainstream groups were going another route, convinced by Clinton's promises and his position papers, as we shall see in the next chapter. Throughout the campaign to harass Bill Clinton, the radical AIDS activists took swings at the mainstream gay and lesbian groups which, one by one, were endorsing him.

Said Mike Petrelis of ACT UP/D.C., "I wish we didn't have to engage in zaps against Clinton, but we have no other choice. Our counterparts at the nation's largest closeted homosexual organization, the Human Rights Campaign Fund, refuse to hold Clinton accountable for his role in promulgating and maintaining this [sodomy] law. When homosexual watchdog organizations turn into Clinton lap dogs, it then becomes necessary for more radical advocates to agitate on behalf of the gay and lesbian community."

In another slam at the mainstream suit-and-tie crowd, ACT UP Presidential Project folks wrote in a March 19, 1992 press release, "What's wrong with this equation? In one day L.A. queers give Clinton $60,000. In ten years Clinton gives Arkansas AIDS community $30,000." The $30,000 is what the Clinton administration allocated to AIDS in 1991-92, the first year it parted with state funds to fight the disease.

In the same release, the Project stated: "As establishment gays jump on the Clinton bandwagon, people living with HIV and AIDS in Arkansas are dying. They are dying because Slick Willie has in his five terms as governor done nothing to fight AIDS." No mincing of words here.

It was no surprise that a split existed in the gay and lesbian community over whether or not to endorse Bill Clinton, the obvious front-runner. The gay/lesbian community has had splits before, and it'll have schisms in the future. It's unavoidable. Especially in a movement that represents such a diverse group of people.

The activists felt that too much was at stake in the presidential race to give away the gay/lesbian community's vote so easily. Thousands of lives were on the line if the new president didn't take the disease seriously enough to halt business as usual and go after it like there was no tomorrow.

The activists in ACT UP and Queer Nation knew what was at stake. They knew all too well how disastrous another four years of neglect would be. And they weren't willing to compromise one bit on what they wanted.

Especially from a slick politician like Bill Clinton, a man the elder statesman of American letters, Gore Vidal, described as less than sincere. Quipped Vidal in the fall 1992 issue of *Out* magazine: "Don't use words like sincere. These words don't apply to people trying to get elected."

5

Wooing the Gay/Lesbian Vote

THERE'S NO DOUBT that Bill Clinton wanted the queer vote. Which is sizeable if you consider that, according to the most commonly held statistic, ten percent of the population of this country is gay or lesbian. If you throw in bisexuals and the transgendered (transsexuals, transvestites), you add on another 20 or more percent. We're talking big numbers here, if that vote were mobilized.

Of course, it never had been, except in about a dozen pockets across the country, places like San Francisco, New York City, Washington, Boston, Philadelphia, Chicago, and Los Angeles. This time around, though, the media attention being paid to the queer vote made it possible to spread the word about candidates throughout the country in an effective manner, not piecemeal, as it had been done before, via gay/lesbian/bisexual newspapers and word-of-mouth.

Suddenly, mainstream newspapers and TV news programs all over the country were talking about the "gay vote" as if it had just sprung overnight from the head of Bill Clinton. No one could miss the news, even in the smallest Southern or Midwestern town. If you were queer anywhere in America in 1992, you knew that something different was happening in terms of the presidential race: Clinton was courting, and the GOP was attacking. Everybody was suddenly taking gays and lesbians seriously because the politicians realized one morning that we vote. It was that simple.

Bill Clinton would have been a fool not to do whatever he could to win the queer vote, whether or not he believed in gay/lesbian or AIDS issues. Whether or not he could shed a tear over military discrimination or the lack of same-sex marriages. Whether or not he ever intended to do anything for queers once he got into office. It was a brilliant strategy to go after this vote. And what could he lose? A few far right votes? He probably wouldn't get those anyway.

For years the polls showed that most Americans favor gay rights. Television sitcoms were championing queer characters now; even the afternoon soaps ran storylines with gay heartbreak, one with a sympathetic teenage gay character. Bill Clinton could safely step out on a limb in terms of gay/lesbian rights issues and still win. Especially if he gained an additional sizeable voting bloc with money.

Money. There was also gay money to be considered. Especially in places like Los Angeles, with all those queers in the entertainment industry. Big Money.

It helped that many in the gay/lesbian establishment, that is, the non-radical, non-ACT UP folks, the suit-and-tie people who work within the system for change, wanted Bill Clinton to be their man. He may not have had Paul Tsongas' impeccable track record, but he was obviously educable on their issues.

Gay Money

The gay money that could be had by Clinton was evident from the start. In May 1992, David Mixner, Clinton's longtime friend and a gay activist in Los Angeles, organized a gala benefit along with Access Now to Gay and Lesbian Equality (ANGLE) at the Palace Nightclub in Hollywood. Touted as the largest gay/lesbian fundraiser for a candidate in history, it raised $100,000. Indeed, it was the biggest chunk of money Clinton, or any other candidate for that matter, ever got from queers at any one time.

ANGLE is a politician's dream with its contributors who, according to *Out* magazine, can pledge $500,000 to the Los Angeles Lesbian and Gay Community Services Center, and a mailing list in the hundreds of thousands.

The Mixner/ANGLE event represented more than simply the first time Clinton gave a major address to a room full of queers.

Remember the TV show, *The Courtship of Eddie's Father*? It depicted a single male (Bill Bixby) raising a child. In this scenario Eddie's father is millions of queer Americans who are being courted by another Bill—Bill Clinton, the persistent suitor. Let's look back at how Clinton wined and dined them on their first real date at the glitzy Palace.

Lights, Camera, Action

Clinton addressed the gathering. "Tonight, I want to talk to you about how we can be one people again—without regard to race or gender or sexual orientation or age or region or income, how we can be one again.

"And those of you who are here tonight, you represent a community of our nation's gifted people whom we have been willing to squander. We can't afford to waste the capacities, the contributions, the hearts, the souls, the minds of the gay and lesbian Americans.

"As soon as the Pentagon issued a study—ironically by a spokesperson who himself was said to be gay—which said that there was no basis in national security for discriminating based on the sexual orientation of Americans who wish to serve in the military, I said I would act on the study. It seemed to me elemental that if a person, a man or woman, wanted to serve their country, they ought to be able to do it. The presumption should be in favor of doing it unless there is some reason not to.

"The Pentagon had a study which said there was no reason not to. The Secretary of Defense, himself obviously personally very uncomfortable at not changing the rules, said it was 'a quaint little rule.' Well, my fellow Americans, we have too much to do to endure 'quaint little rules.' "

Obviously aware of what an important issue AIDS is for a predominantly white gay male audience, Clinton addressed it with passion that night. Acknowledging that over a million Americans are HIV-positive, he said, "When it comes to AIDS, there should be a Manhattan Project [author's note: a national summit of experts; forum used during World War II to develop the atom bomb]. One person should be in charge. One person who can cut across all the departments and agencies, who has the president's ear and the president's arm. One person who can make sure that we begin by implementing all those recommendations [of the President's Commission on AIDS] and those two commission reports now gathering dust in Washington, D.C."

Clinton also pledged that "someone who is HIV-positive, but also has a positive attitude" would speak at the Democratic National Convention.

As he was wrapping up, Clinton said, "And now before I leave, I want to say something which is not part of a political program. I just want to thank the gay and lesbian community for your courage and your commitment and your service in the face of the terror of AIDS. When no one was offering a helping hand, and when it was dark and lonely, you did not withdraw, but instead you reached out to others." Choking with emotion, Clinton continued, "If I could, if I could wave my arm for those of you that are HIV-positive and make it go away tomorrow, I would do it, so help me God I would. If I gave up my race for the White House and everything else, I would do that."

Pander Bear?

Was Bill Clinton playing "pander bear?" Was Clinton "willing to say anything, to do anything to get elected," as Tsongas once described it?

The *Washington Post* the next day concluded: "There was a time when those words out of Clinton's mouth might have seemed the ultimate in pandering. But on this night from the tone of his voice and the look on his face, many in the audience said they were inclined to believe him."

Bill Clinton had done a convincing job with that first speech to the gay/lesbian community. And with Roberta Achtenberg and David Mixner behind him that night, how could he not win the gay/lesbian/bisexual vote?

Mixner told the gathering, "We have all come a long way tonight. No one handed us this event tonight … we

earned it, inch by inch, step by step, moment by moment."

Said *Los Angeles Times* writer Ronald Brownstein the
next day in the lead of his article on the benefit: "Almost
anything Arkansas Governor Bill Clinton said to the audience of gay and lesbian activists who turned out at a
fund-raiser for his campaign in Hollywood seemed less
important than the simple fact that he was there."

The *Los Angeles Times* photograph accompanying
the article was flawless: it showed a smiling Clinton
standing before the crowd, like a rock star before his
fans, in this case the suit-and-tie crowd, who were reach-
ing to touch him. Almost thirty years ago, these same
men might have been at the foot of the stage where Judy
Garland was singing *Over the Rainbow* or John Lennon
and Paul McCartney were singing *I Wanna Hold Your
Hand.* It looks like that kind of adulation.

Bill Clinton didn't sing a song that night, but he sure
wanted to take them over the rainbow and hold their
hands—and it didn't hurt that those hands were filled
with money.

The Democratic presidential contender didn't stop
his courtship in May. He continued wooing queers
throughout the primary, after the convention and right
up to the election. He even answered questionnaires
from several gay/AIDS groups, giving stock liberal answers. And as often happens during a courtship, he
made a lot of promises.

Clinton also generated a lot of paperwork on gay/
lesbian and AIDS issues. Which is progress, considering
the scant amount other presidential candidates have
said about queer issues.

Mainstream queers wanted to be seduced by Bill
Clinton. He didn't have to "work hard for his money."

Hillary Clinton on AIDS

Hillary Clinton got into the act in April, giving an exclusive interview to the *Bay Area Reporter* via the paper's Los Angeles freelance reporter, Karen Ocamb. While on a visit to AIDS Project Los Angeles, Mrs. Clinton talked about her former colleague, Dan Bradley, an out gay man with whom she worked at Legal Services Corporation, an agency that helps the poor.

Remembering Bradley's battle against AIDS (which he lost in 1987), she said, "He chose to live out his last years with the same level of intensity that he had lived his whole life and when somebody does that, you feel like it's been a life that should be celebrated and that's what I think most of his friends felt. He wanted for all of us to be committed to what he had fought for his entire life," she continued. "He taught me a lot."

Gay Endorsements

Clinton's work with the gay/lesbian community paid off. In April, openly gay United States Representative Barney Frank (Democrat from Massachusetts) made a plea for gay support of Clinton at New York's Gay and Lesbian Community Center. Frank said that the attacks on Clinton from the ACT UP Presidential Project were "suicidal. How will we change public policy if we don't get Bush out of the White House?"

In early May Clinton won the endorsement of openly gay United States Representative Gerry Studds (D-Massachusetts) after the presidential hopeful addressed the Democratic caucus of the House. Now he had the backing of the only two out queers in Congress.

"It was refreshing after twelve years and two presidents who were barely even able to say 'AIDS,' much less show a real commitment to battle it," said Studds.

The country's gay/lesbian newspapers also endorsed him in droves before their states' primaries.

Perhaps the most revealing of these endorsements came from the Missouri-based *News-Telegraph*. Acknowledging that Arkansas as well as Missouri and Kansas are conservative states, the editor wrote in June, echoing the kind of apologizing some queers would do for the man from Little Rock: "In fact, it is our own knowledge of Missouri political life that makes us understand precisely how a state leader might well blossom when emerging on the national stage."

For other gay/lesbian papers, the issue wasn't that Clinton as president might be more progressive than Clinton the governor of a conservative Southern state. The most succinct statement of the other point of view was penned in an editorial by *Bay Times* publisher/editor Kim Corsaro: "The fight against George Bush is more than an election. It's our lives."

Larry Kramer was firm in his endorsement of the man from Little Rock. "It's incumbent upon all gay people to vote for Clinton because he offers the best hope," Kramer told QW. "He's very smart and his wife is very smart, and I think he's genuinely concerned."

Kramer will always best be known as the author of the hit play *The Normal Heart*, the first no-holds-barred history of the early years of the AIDS epidemic. So his endorsement held a lot of weight with many in the AIDS activist community.

The Human Rights Campaign Fund came out in support of Clinton in early June. It was the first time in its 12-year history that the political lobby had endorsed a presidential candidate. Laura Altschul, co-chair of HRCF's board of directors, explained to Boston's *Bay*

Windows, a gay/lesbian newspaper, one of the reasons for her group's nod to the Arkansas governor: "Clinton has made it clear that he will fight to end discrimination against lesbian and gay Americans and will push for our health care concerns."

That same month, Clinton made the news with pro-gay statements at several appearances. On the CBS program *This Morning*, Clinton reiterated his commitment to hire an AIDS czar and implement the recommendations of the Presidential Commission on AIDS, adding that he would "fund the Ryan White Act." That act provides federal money to states for AIDS care work. The amount of money is determined by the number of cases in that state.

In the area of sex discrimination, Clinton said, "I'm going to make it clear that we will not tolerate sexual harassment in the federal workplace. And I'm going to appoint people to positions in government, both women and men, who will speak out against gender bias and sexual discrimination and will work against it and will live and act against it."

At a Broadway fundraiser for his campaign, Clinton, wearing the red ribbon that symbolizes concern for AIDS, repeated his promise to appoint the AIDS czar; he also said that he would make sure a person with AIDS spoke at the Democratic Convention.

And at an MTV Q & A session featuring people 18-to-24 years old, the presidential candidate told a gay film student, Minh Tran, that he opposed the military's policy on barring queers. Asked by MTV reporter Tabatha Soren why the Arkansas sodomy law was still on the books, he replied, "Because I'm only a governor, I'm not a legislator."

Clinton: Governor with an Eye on the Presidency

But a governor can recommend and push legislation to the state legislature. He had more influence than Bill Clinton gave himself credit for. Clinton clearly didn't want credit for any gubernatorial influence when it came to certain issues, such as AIDS and sodomy.

What happened in Arkansas with both AIDS issues and the sodomy law is obvious if you remember that Clinton suffered a defeat in 1980 after his first term as governor. Learning from that lesson, the Clinton who re-emerged as governor after a two-year absence was more cautious in his approach. Cautious enough not to rock any boats on controversial issues, if he didn't have to, and to keep the governorship until his bid for the presidency. If sodomy is still controversial in New York City, imagine how it plays down on the farm in Arkansas. Clinton isn't stupid.

As Hastings Wyman, Jr., editor of the *Southern Political Report*, told the *Advocate* (January 26, 1993): "My guess is that Clinton would have favored a more liberal position on the sodomy law, but as a pragmatic politician he realized that he could not have stopped it and that it would only hurt his political future."

Major AIDS Address

Winding down his courtship, Clinton gave a major address on AIDS in New Jersey a week before the election, an unprecedented and risky move. It was the fulfillment of a campaign promise to AIDS activists, many of whom doubted he would ever go through with it. The speech was drafted by Ben Schatz, executive director of the American Association of Physicians for Human Rights, a national gay/lesbian group.

Of course, the ever-cautious Clinton gave it late in the afternoon, at a time when it wouldn't make it to the network evening news.

"We must remember, for all of its terror and far reach, it is still a disease," Clinton said. "It is not vengeance or punishment or just-desserts; it is an illness. We have fought illnesses before, and we must fight this one now."

This is pretty much the way it went throughout the campaign. Bill Clinton was asked, Bill Clinton responded. Every once in a while, he goofed, said something too moderate, or maybe downright conservative, as we'll see in the next chapter.

Promises, Promises

Bill Clinton made a number of promises to the gay and lesbian community during the campaign for the presidency. Here's what he said he'd do in the area of **gay/lesbian rights**:

- Issue an executive order ending military discrimination against gays and lesbians.
- Issue an executive order ending discrimination in federal employment.
- Support the federal gay/lesbian rights bill, should it ever pass Congress (unlikely, I think, even with more sponsors than ever before) and arrive on his desk.
- Appoint out gays and lesbians to his administration.

As for AIDS, he repeatedly said he would:

- Appoint an AIDS czar to oversee the country's policies on the disease.
- Implement the recommendations of the President's Commission on AIDS, ignored by President George Bush.
- Oppose AIDS discrimination.
- Develop a Manhattan-type project (similar to the one that developed the atomic bomb) to seek a cure for AIDS.

Feeding the Clinton Coffers

Overall, Clinton did exceptionally well in the campaign, considering how new this courting of the gay/lesbian vote was for both the Democratic party and the man himself. He certainly kept the bigwigs in the mainstream gay/lesbian movement happy. And they fed his campaign coffers.

By September 1992 David Mixner, who was a National Executive Committee member at the time, was telling Chicago's *Windy City Times* that queers had contributed at least two million dollars to the Clinton campaign. He cautioned that this amount only reflected money clearly identified as queer. An additional $200,000 was raised by HRCF's Presidential Project by September. The next two months would see a wealth of other fundraisers in the gay/lesbian community. By the end of the campaign the two million dollar figure would almost double.

The Democratic National Committee even set up a special post office box just for gay/lesbian contributors who wanted to make sure the Democrats knew the sexual orientation of their dollars.

Toward the end of the race, the *Wall Street Journal* (October 30, 1992) summed it this way: "The gay community has emerged as one of Bill Clinton's most important cash constituencies." The article was accompanied by a "Gay Giving" sidebar with the names of queer political action groups donating to candidates.

The *Wall Street Journal* quotes Clinton Campaign Finance Director Rahm Emanuel as saying, "From the very beginning, financial support from the gay community has been instrumental." And to make sure people got the message loud and clear, the paper quotes Rich Tafel of the National Federation of Log Cabin Clubs as saying that "Gay Republicans have not been writing checks to Republicans."

The article also made it clear that it didn't hurt Bill Clinton any that the right-wing attacked gays and lesbians. "Support crystallized overnight with Pat Buchanan's speech [at the Republican Convention]," Mixner said. "It created a voting bloc and tripled the money."

Another way that the GOP strategy of scapegoating queers backfired.

Mainstream Gays Support Clinton

Clearly, mainstream gays and lesbians were not taking chances this time around. They were desperate to get George Bush and his right-wing cronies out of office at any cost. Bill Clinton was their knight in shining armor. No doubt about that.

In the Castro, queer Democrats regularly set up tables with Clinton literature and buttons. Clinton posters were the most popular item on the block and in the neighborhood.

Even the *Washington Post* on September 28, 1992 noticed the overwhelming support Clinton had in the country's most visible queer neighborhood. "Gay people are going ape—they're going crazy over Clinton," Castro gay activist Dennis Peron told the *Post*. "Every single house on my street has a Clinton-Gore sign."

He wasn't exaggerating.

By the fall of 1992, a hot selling item in the Castro, especially at A Different Light Bookstore, San Francisco's only queer book venue, was a tee-shirt with Clinton's and Gore's heads pasted on shirtless male torsos, their arms around each other, perfectly defined pectorals clearly evident: the fantasy white gay boys. Printed across their crotches in huge letters: "Clinton Gore '92." The picture also popped up on postcards and magnets, the work of an unknown computer artist(s). Though I'm sure the Clinton folks did not endorse the photograph, nothing was ever said about it. No official denouncements. Clinton's campaign people were keeping the lid on this one. They could always feign ignorance, if asked about it. Meanwhile, that photo didn't hurt the popularity of Clinton and his running mate in the gay white male community.

It was more obvious every day that Eddie's father was winning: the object of desire was surrendering to his will.

6

Clinton's Slip Was Showing

IN GAY MALE CAMP, we use an expression when someone makes a mistake or inadvertently reveals something that's not supposed to be revealed: "Your slip is showing." Obviously it derives from an embarrassing situation for the traditional woman: her slip showing from under her dress.

Sometimes when it came to queer issues, Bill Clinton's slip was showing big time.

Early on in the primary, Clinton aroused the concern of the gay/lesbian community when he expressed reservations about the federal gay/lesbian rights bill.

In responding to an HRCF question about whether he would sign and enforce the bill, Clinton wrote: "I believe that the portions of the bill dealing with the hiring of secular employees by religious organizations, and those concerned with the enforcement of non-numerical affirmative action, need further consideration and development. If Congress passed a bill resolving these issues, I would sign it."

He also said on the same questionnaire that he does not believe same-sex couples have "the right to marry and enjoy the same legal and tax benefits as heterosexual couples."

The responses caused a lot of fallout in the queer press. In a letter to Randy Klose, co-chair of the board of HRCF, Clinton clarified his position.

"I am a strong supporter of civil rights for gays and lesbians, as I am for all Americans," he wrote. "As president, I will sign the federal gay civil rights bill as long as the final version addresses my concerns on two matters, which I believe will help facilitate the passage of the bill."

Not backing down from his concerns about affirmative action and the exemption of religious organizations, Clinton said that they do not "reflect on my fundamental commitment to civil rights for gays and lesbians."

By the end of the campaign, he was promising to sign the federal legislation without any caveats.

Clinton Slips In Portland

In July Clinton participated in a Portland television taping opposite Scott Lively, spokesperson for the Oregon Citizens Alliance, the group behind the anti-gay initiative in that state.

Clinton and Lively had a little back-and-forth about gay/lesbian rights. During that exchange, Clinton said that the Boy Scouts of America, an organization that discriminates against gay men, "are a private organization and, as such, they ought to have a right to whatever rules they want. That's different from the United States government."

Lively then asked, "Would you then support the teaching of homosexuality as a normal and natural lifestyle to children in public schools?"

To which Clinton replied, "That's not what I'm talking about … I'm not talking about embracing a lifestyle that you may think is wrong or even immoral. I'm talking about the existence of American men and women and their ability to live their lives and fulfill their potential and make a contribution to the rest of us."

Was Clinton backing down on gay issues? It's obvious he was trying to straddle the fence by using the phrase "I'm not talking about embracing a lifestyle." Why not simply say, "Yes, children should hear that homosexuality is perfectly normal, because it is."

But that was not Bill Clinton's style—especially if he wanted to be elected president by maintaining a centrist position.

Asked about the TV taping, Mixner told Pittsburgh's gay/lesbian newspaper *Out*, "When you take it in context, I don't think he said anything that takes away from his strong support on our issues. Is he perfect? Of course not, but who is?"

Mixner, a longtime activist on many fronts, including civil rights for blacks, was obviously determined to keep believing in Clinton. Mixner, who's in his forties, participated in lunch-counter sit-ins in the South, and was beaten at the Democratic National Convention in Chicago in 1968. He met Bill Clinton around 1969 at Oxford.

"I've known Bill and Hillary since the anti-war days of the late 60's," he told the *Washington Blade* in July. "I came out to them 16 years ago."

Now he was Clinton's point man in the queer community. And determined to get Bush out of office: "One hundred eight friends dead from AIDS. I feel this [Bush] administration committed genocide in killing my community."

Mixner was in it for the finish.

The Oregon Measure: A Divisive Issue

The Oregon measure caused problems for Clinton on more than one occasion. Asked about the anti-gay/lesbian initiative by a Portland reporter after a political rally, Clinton said, "I think it's basically a divisive measure. My own view is that this should be a country that is free of discrimination."

If only he had kept his mouth shut while he was ahead. Clinton added: "But I don't think there should be affirmative steps to promote the homosexual lifestyle."

Oops.

Not only were queers upset at the quote, but also at the fact that Clinton didn't mention the anti-gay/lesbian measure in his speech at the rally. This despite the fact that gays and lesbians held up "No on 9" signs to prompt him to say something.

And, of course, they were angry that his quote sounded like rhetoric from a fundamentalist pamphlet against gay/lesbian rights. The argument against "promotion of the homosexual lifestyle" has been used against the NEA, gay rights legislation, AIDS funding, adoption by queer parents; in short, just about every battle the gay/lesbian movement has fought.

Mixner was upset about the controversy that followed Clinton's remark. "I think it was a knee-jerk response," he told San Diego's *Update*. "And I think we're doing [Clinton] a great disservice. We ought to have a little more time and trust—this man has earned that much from us. This is ridiculous."

Some gay and lesbian activists expressed concern that the reporter may have bungled the quote. Which does happen. After all, they said, Clinton wasn't prone to using religious right-wing jargon.

Clinton was again clearly playing it safely by not being too vocal in his opposition to Measure 9. He knew this opposition could be used against his campaign in a big way by a well-organized anti-gay/lesbian lobby in that state. The call on the initiative was close. He wasn't taking chances.

A month later, during a return trip to Oregon, Clinton did address the issue of Measure 9 at a rally. "I ask you to send a message to America by resoundingly defeating [Measure] 9. Vote no."

Was he learning from his mistakes? It seemed so. Or was he merely trying to keep the gay/lesbian vote from falling apart? Clinton needed it intact; he needed to get as much of it as he could.

Clinton Didn't Court Non-Whites

One thing he didn't do, though, is court the gay and lesbian vote in the communities of color throughout this country. Another instance of his slip showing.

Sandra Lowe, a black attorney who heads New York Governor Mario Cuomo's Office of Lesbian and Gay Concerns, told *Out* magazine after the convention that she didn't know of any Clinton outreach efforts in the black gay/lesbian community.

However, she wasn't making an issue out of it yet. "Too much is riding on this election, so nobody wants to say anything bad," she told the magazine. "We'll deal with it after the election."

San Francisco activist Bryant Kong sees the question of Clinton's lack of outreach to queers of color in context of the larger picture. "The outreach that people of color and dispossessed groups generally get from the mainstream Democratic Party is an outreach of tokenism and white liberal guilt," said Kong. "The model that we got for Americans with the Clinton-Gore ticket is the successful white baby boomer," said Kong. "And if you're a successful, non-white, non-straight baby boomer then you're fine, too. But what if you're not successful, then where are you?"

Clearly you didn't count.

Bill Clinton couldn't—and didn't—ignore the upwardly mobile white gay male community. That's where the money was. That's where the powerbrokers were who could deliver Bill Clinton the "gay vote" on a silver platter.

That's where the folks were who would shake their heads whenever anyone mentioned a slip showing. A reverse of those hapless fairy tale characters who saw the emperor in clothes when he clearly had none. "What slip? Is Bill Clinton wearing a slip?" A lot of people in the gay/lesbian community merely laughed at this question. "Slip? He's not wearing a slip. You must be thinking of Madonna."

7

After the Election

The mood on Castro Street on the evening of November 3, 1992 was beyond comparison. Victory was in the air even before it was announced that Bill Clinton had won the presidency of the United States.

"Ding dong the witch is dead," people sang, referring, of course, to George Bush. The reign of terror was over. Twelve years of loved ones dying. Twelve years of setbacks in civil rights legislation. Twelve years of wondering whether tomorrow the concentration camps would open and gay men and lesbians would begin "disappearing."

Via outdoor speakers, celebrants heard Clinton's victory speech, the second paragraph of which mentioned AIDS in a list of concerns "too long ignored." There was also talk of the diversity of America, which many took to include queers, though gays and lesbians were not mentioned by name.

There was dancing in the street that night on Castro. Being the world's most renowned queer ghetto, Castro Street is often the site of instant demonstrations or celebrations in reaction to news events from around the country. When California Governor Pete Wilson finally signed a watered-down version of AB 101, the state's gay/

lesbian rights employment bill, queers gathered in the Castro to party.

Sometimes, it seems, the parties are more self-indulgence than anything else. Wilson's signing of a skeletal gay rights bill was hardly cause for celebration. Though it's perfectly understandable that we would party that night—for a disenfranchised group, every crumb seems like the whole enchilada.

The same could be said for Bill Clinton's election. After all, what had been won? A lot of promises? Words are cheap; action is the real test of the man. And action would be months away, if ever. A president had been supported on blind faith alone. After all, there was still the fact that he was a centrist; there was also the very real matter of his Arkansas record. For many there is nothing to do except go on the blind faith that he will do right by the queer community now.

Everything's Hunky-Dory

On that chilly November night in the Castro, everything seemed right: a pro-gay president was in office; the anti-gay/lesbian initiatives in Oregon and Portland, Maine were defeated; more out gay and lesbian candidates had won office around the country, bringing the total up to a record 75; and San Francisco's own Roberta Achtenberg was with Clinton in Little Rock to celebrate his election. There was even talk that Achtenberg would get an appointment to the Clinton administration as a payback for her work on his behalf.

A headline in *USA Today* the week before said: "Millions of Gays mobilizing for the 'vote of our lives.' " That's just what we did. And it paid off royally. On election night, it seemed the world was made for us queers.

We may as well have echoed the Supremes: "There's no stopping us now."

Or is there?

Reality check: the battle in Colorado was lost. By a 53–47 percent margin, fundamentalists succeeded in nixing gay/lesbian rights, making it the first state to officially declare queers second-class citizens. And the year-old Tampa, Florida gay/lesbian rights measure was overturned by a 58–42 percent vote. The right had enough of a consensus to move forward with its new anti-queer agenda. Even the anti-abortion organization Operation Rescue was beginning to use queers as a convenient issue to raise funds.

But for the crowds in the Castro, Colorado and Florida were indeed many miles away that night.

80 Percent for Clinton

According to an average based on five different polls, the gay vote went 80 percent for Bill Clinton, 9.6 percent for Bush, and 7.8 percent for independent candidate Ross Perot.

This average is based on polls by Overlooked Opinions (with a database of 35,000 gays/lesbians); gay/lesbian news publications (10 papers and magazines in 10 different cities, each of which inserted voter-survey cards into copies of their publications); TV network exit polls conducted by Voter Research & Surveys at 300 precincts; Mason/Dixon polls commissioned by the *Washington Blade*; and gay cluster surveys at 59 precincts in 11 cities identified as having large queer voting blocks.

The Overlook Opinions poll put the gay vote for Clinton at the highest: 89 percent; the gay cluster precincts put it at the lowest: 74 percent. In either case, the pro-Clinton vote was well over two-thirds.

Chicago's *Outlines*, a gay/lesbian monthly, published a chart showing a state-by-state gay/lesbian/bisexual breakdown of votes for Bill Clinton. The estimated figures were based on CNN exit poll data. It was compiled by GayNet News Service and *Outlines'* Publisher/Managing Editor Tracy Baim.

That chart was the first of its kind. A solid indication that the gay vote is here to stay. How can future election analysts not count the queer vote? How can they ignore the results of this race?

According to the *Outlines* chart, the votes split like this:

State	Clinton	Bush
California	346,683	43,442
Colorado*	45,087	7,250
D.C.	13,414	258
Florida	147,733	27,791
Massachusetts	94,681	10,459
Michigan	133,796	20,632
New York	233,769	29,137
Oregon**	37,809	5,127
Pennsylvania	160,193	23,117
Texas	164,107	31,984
Wyoming	4,886	1,034

*Where the anti-gay Amendment 2 passed
**Where the anti-gay Measure 9 failed

In every state, Clinton beat out George Bush among gay/lesbian voters. Adding the results from all 50 states, the total number of gay/lesbian votes for Bill Clinton: 3,148,447 to George Bush's 496,176. Altogether, Clinton received 43.7 million votes in the election. If you do a simple division on those numbers, the gay/lesbian vote represented 14 percent.

The *Washington Blade* figured that Clinton received 6.3 million of the votes from the nation's gay and lesbian community. The paper based its figure on a survey of 1,000 readers of the queer press in 10 cities.

No matter how you look at it, a large number of queers pulled that lever for Bill Clinton.

The Right-Wing Strategy Failed

The right-wing strategy of attacking Clinton's support for queers failed. America didn't buy it, either at the Republican Convention or at the polls a few months later. Anti-queer bigotry sold only in some instances where it was specifically aimed at rights laws: for example, Colorado.

The situation was clear two months before the election as far as the anti-queer attacks working to defeat the man from Little Rock.

A *Newsweek* poll, featured as a front-cover story, showed that more than half of Americans were in favor of most gay/lesbian issues, except for marriage and adoption.

According to the *Newsweek* poll: 78 percent believe queers should have equal rights in job opportunities; 41 percent believe homosexuality is an acceptable alternative lifestyle; 51 percent believe queers are not a threat to the family; 43 percent have a friend who is gay. Half or more believe queers should be hired as salespeople, members of the president's cabinet, in the armed forces, as doctors, high school teachers, elementary-school teachers, and clergy.

Still more surprising answers: 67 percent approve of health insurance for gay spouses; 70 percent in inheritance rights for gay spouses; 58 percent in social security for gay spouses. Yet only 35 percent favor legally sanctioned same-sex marriages, and 32 percent approve of adoption rights for queer couples.

As for Clinton, 44 percent felt that his position on gay rights was "about right."

Great Day for Queers

The national gay/lesbian groups gloated the day after the election. And they had every reason to. The right-wing forces of hatred had indeed been sent a strong message by the victory of a pro-gay candidate.

Said HRCF's Tim McFeeley in a press release the following day: "This is a great day for lesbian and gay Americans and a great victory for all Americans. The election of our lives is over. Never before have our issues been at the top of the agenda, issues such as AIDS, discrimination and our right to live as equal Americans. The American public have rejected the calls of bigotry that were heard at the Republican Convention in Houston, and in overwhelming numbers they have given their support to candidates who will stand with us when the votes are taken in Congress."

HRCF deployed some 20 workers around the country in the final weeks before the election to "mobilize Campaign Fund members as volunteers in the Clinton/Gore campaign and in critical senate and congressional races." Three of these members worked in Oregon against Measure 9.

Altogether, HRCF contributed $717,000 to candidates in the 1992 election. That's $200,000 more than in 1990.

Daniel Bross, director of the AIDS Action Council, told the *Washington Blade*, "I think this is the breakthrough we have been waiting for in the fight against AIDS. We have every reason to be optimistic and hopeful that the president-elect will address AIDS as a health-care issue and not as a political or moral issue, which is the way it's been treated for the last 12 years."

Rite of Passage

NGLTF declared in its press release and at a press conference the following day: "On the whole, most gay men and lesbians are celebrating the national election outcomes with a sense that a historic moment in the gay movement has been reached."

NGLTF's then-director Vaid said: "This election marks a rite of passage for the gay and lesbian civil rights movement—passage from the margin to center, from political pariah to welcome partner, from ignorance and fear to broader understanding. We stand as a people at a turning point—for the first time in American political history, lesbians and gay men will serve as equal partners in the governance of our country.

"This year," Vaid continued, "we delivered something we had only claimed as a potentiality before: we delivered a crucial voting bloc that helped elect the next president of the United States."

As for the Republican right, Vaid said, "[It's] appeal to narrow definition of family values failed. The use of homophobia in the presidential election—by Buchanan and the Bush campaign—failed. The spectacle of a Republican Party led far afield by the extremist-right turned off significant numbers of the American electorate. The clearest example of this failure came in Septem-

ber of 1992 when President Bush and Vice President
Quayle felt compelled to falsely announce that their Administration had a policy of non-discrimination based
on sexual orientation."

Transition Document

NGLTF released, at that same press conference on the day
after the election, its presidential transition document
for Bill Clinton. The 11-page, single-spaced document
calls on Clinton to fulfill his promises to the queer community—and more. It asks for "presidential leadership
to create a climate of tolerance and respect for the diversity of human life."

Seven areas were targeted for Clinton's attention:
presidential leadership; civil rights; AIDS, health and well
being; anti-gay and lesbian violence; freedom of expression; the District of Columbia; and diverse families.

Presidential Leadership

NGLTF asks that Clinton set up a meeting with national
gay/lesbian leaders within his first one hundred days,
ideally to coincide with the April 25, 1993 National
March on Washington for Lesbian/Gay/Bisexual Rights;
that he recruit and hire out queers in his new administration; and that he veto anti-gay/lesbian legislation.

Civil Rights

Civil rights includes several areas. The president should,
according to the NGLTF document, issue an executive
order on the 50th anniversary (January 1993) of the original directive barring gay/lesbian participation in the

military to reverse that policy. He should also sign an executive order prohibiting discrimination in federal employment and contracts based on sexual orientation; request congressional hearings on the magnitude of gay/lesbian discrimination in employment, housing, public accommodations, credit and federally assisted opportunities; and endorse and work for the Civil Rights Amendment Act.

Finally, Clinton should issue an executive order barring the denial of security clearances based on sexual orientation; issue an order repealing the military sodomy code; and condemn human rights violations against queers in other countries.

AIDS, Health and Well-being

Five recommendations address AIDS specifically: implement the recommendations of the National Commission on AIDS; ensure that health care reform includes funding for AIDS services and protects people with the disease; provide adequate funds for the search for a cure; support honest HIV prevention campaigns; and lead the battle against discrimination against those with HIV and AIDS.

In the area of health and well-being, the new president must implement the 1989 Report of the Secretary's Task Force on Youth Suicide and commission the Department of Health and Human Services, which drafted the study, to conduct more.

That report concludes that up to 30 percent of all teen suicides in the United States occurs among young people struggling to come to terms with their sexual orientation. Unfortunately, the report fell victim to politics—the right forced it onto the proverbial shelf where it now collects dust.

The other concern in this area is lesbian health. NGLTF wants a director for the Office of Women's Health at the National Institute of Health who will focus on lesbian health care needs; and a president who will support federal legislative initiatives only if they are inclusive of the health care needs of lesbians and all women.

Anti-Gay/Lesbian Violence

NGLTF demands funding for the FBI's hate crimes statistic collection effort to attain accurate information on the extent of these incidents. It also wants the president to direct federal agencies to study and remedy the problem of bias crimes; to support the efforts of school agencies and community-based groups that are combating hate crimes; to direct federal agencies to commit resources to ensure that programs serving victims of hate crimes receive federal funding.

Freedom of Expression

Two recommendations are proposed to address freedom of expression: the opposition of censorship at the National Endowment for the Arts; and disbanding of the National Obscenity Enforcement Unit, which uses federal funds to crusade against so-called obscene materials. In the past, this has often meant targeting material with homosexual content. As far as the activists are concerned, it has to go the way of the dinosaur.

The District of Columbia

As for the District of Columbia, NGLTF wants it to be the 51st state to remove congressional interference into its local affairs. At present, Congress has jurisdiction over the District, which has meant, for queers, that pro-gay/lesbian legislation passed there is always in danger of being vetoed by that body.

Diverse Families

Last, but not least, the president should convene a Commission on Family Diversity within the first two years of his administration to review the patterns of change within family structures and provide recommendations to support the needs of traditional and non-traditional families.

Pulling No Punches

The tone of the HRCF and NGLTF releases after the election were not confrontational at all. In contrast, the release from the national office of the April 25 March on Washington was headlined: "President Clinton's Honeymoon is 95 Days."

Pulling no punches, the release states: "On April 25th, the president can have one million grateful supporters or one million angry citizens on his doorstep."

The last national queer march on D.C., in 1987, drew about 650,000. The 1993 march is expected to exceed a million, making it one of the largest to hit the nation's capital.

In the weeks following the election, all eyes were glued to President-Elect Bill Clinton as he went about the business of putting his new administration together. Within the first few weeks after the election, the signs were hopeful: 13 out queers—a record number—were included on his transition team.

The transition team queers included Bob Hattoy,

who spoke on AIDS at the convention; Tim Westmore-
land, aide to Representative Henry Waxman; David
Geffen, the record company mogul who was recently
named Man of the Year by the national gay publication,
The Advocate, for his work as an AIDS fundraiser; and
Chai Feldblum, a lobbyist who helped win the Americans with Disabilities Act, which addresses the needs of
persons with disabilities, including those with AIDS.

David Mixner told the *San Francisco Examiner* (December 20, 1992): "This is historic for us, having
[openly] gay people on the transition team. It's never
been done before."

By the beginning of December, the transition team
prepared a paper on AIDS as well as separate ones on
strategies for passing a federal gay/lesbian rights bill and
the lifting of the military ban. The papers were sent to
Clinton for his review.

But Bill Clinton also showed signs of waffling on the
military issue. Instead of an executive order ending the
ban on queers, he seemed to favor something less defini-
tive, less confrontational, perhaps less controversial. He
was now talking about forming a commission. It did not
bode well.

Disappointing Appointment

Nor did it bode well that the first crop of Clinton appointments included no out lesbians or gay men. It did
include the naming of Donna Shalala to the post of Secretary of Health and Human Services. Shalala, chancel-
lor of the University of Wisconsin at Madison, has a
lukewarm record of supporting gay/lesbian rights at that
institution.

Shalala spent her first few weeks as a nominee denying rumors that she is a lesbian. Clinton had no comment. Said Shalala: "Have I lived an alternative lifestyle? The answer is no."

As for Shalala's record on gay and lesbian rights in Wisconsin, some activists interviewed after her nomination expressed reservation about her sincerity on their issues. Cited was her refusal to support a move to ban the campus ROTC because of its policy of excluding gays and lesbians.

The ROTC policy flies in the face of Wisconsin state, city and university rules on non-discrimination. A number of colleges throughout the country have banned ROTC for this very reason: it's difficult to reconcile a non-discrimination policy that includes sexual orientation with a military that excludes queers.

Shalala is on record against the ROTC policy. She told Wisconsin freelance writer Jamakaya in a *San Francisco Sentinel* piece: "I share [the students'] frustration and I can see that the policies are inconsistent. But I do not have executive authority on this issue."

Gay and lesbian students disagreed. "Shalala never brought her influence to bear on these things," Brad Berkland of the Ten Percent Society, a campus gay/lesbian group, told the *Sentinel*. "She talks a lot about very progressive ideas, but there's been very little action."

Jane Vanderbosch of the Madison gay/lesbian group United summed up a lot of queer student sentiment when she described Shalala as "a real disappointment."

Other activists said that in recommending the development of a program to "persuade the Congress and the military ... to end discriminatory practices," rather than calling for an outright ban, she took the most "realistic view of how to achieve change." They say that this way she avoided confronting the Republican-dominated Board of Regents.

Berkland told the *Washington Blade* that Shalala "is publicly supportive of the gay community on campus, but it's hard to point to anything she's really done for us. She did sign onto an ad discouraging military bias, but beyond statements to the press, we've not seen anything come of it."

At the press conference where Clinton announced her appointment, Shalala outlined her priorities. "The initial challenges of Health and Human Services, which the governor outlined, are to build a national consensus for quality health care to aggressively and strategically attack the AIDS epidemic. ..."

That AIDS was mentioned so prominently in her remarks could be a hopeful sign. Of course, it could also be one of many good intentions that will never be realized.

Other Appointments

For weeks after Clinton made his first appointments, reports surfaced in the gay/lesbian press about the appointees' views on queer issues. Seen as particularly hopeful was Secretary of Defense nominee Representative Les Aspin, a Democrat from Wisconsin.

NGLTF's Peri Jude Radecic was quoted in *Bay Windows* as saying that Aspin "has done a lot of things behind the scenes." But Aspin has never co-sponsored the federal gay/lesbian rights bill, and has a less than perfect voting record on queer issues. Still, Radecic said that "his staff has been really good and supportive."

A more recent nominee is San Francisco Supervisor Roberta Achtenberg to the position of Assistant Secretary for Fair Housing, Equal Opportunity and Enforcement in the Department of Housing and Urban Development.

Top-Level Appointments Unlikely

Can queers realistically expect any out gay or lesbian appointments in top-level positions? It's unlikely. My guess is that whatever appointments are made will be low-profile ones, so that they don't come under the scrutiny of the public.

Clinton the moderate does not want to be perceived as stuck in the back pocket of the queer movement, one of the many "special interest" groups attached to the Democratic Party. After all, Clinton was one of the Democrats behind the Democratic Leadership Council, which believed that pandering to special interest groups in 1984 and 1988 cost the party the White House.

As Brian Lunde, a former director of the Democratic National Committee, told the *San Francisco Chronicle* (December 24, 1992): "If it looks like these groups can get a foothold with pressure, that would hurt [Clinton]. He doesn't want to have the same problem Walter Mondale had in the 1984 campaign, where he is perceived by the public, fairly or unfairly, as a tool of the Democratic interest groups."

Added Stuart Eizenstat, a D.C. attorney who served as Jimmy Carter's domestic policy adviser, "The best way to deal with these groups is to let them know if that is the attitude they are going to take, they are not going to get in the White House."

That's the message Clinton sent when he attacked feminists who were upset early on in the appointments process because they didn't think he named enough women to posts in his administration. An angry Clinton fired back that he wouldn't hold to quotas. Yet women were an important constituency he wooed during his election. If he doesn't feel some commitment to give a number of appointments to women, then what can queers bank on? The fact that a few gay friends of his died of AIDS? Hardly.

If his behavior in Arkansas is any indication of things to come, Bill Clinton is not going to leave the campaign trail during his first term in the White House. It's obvious he intends to be a two-term chief executive.

I'll bet that's the primary motivating force behind his actions these next four years.

ACT UP Likes Elders

The best news about the appointments is Clinton's nominee for United States Surgeon General: Dr. Joycelyn Elders of the Arkansas Health Department. Even ACT UP likes Elders, who supported condom distribution in the Arkansas public schools.

Said ACT UP/D.C.'s Mike Petrelis: "ACT UP's endorsement of Elders' appointment should not be viewed as the kiss of death." What it should be seen as, he said, is the beginning of a working relationship between health officials and those with AIDS.

Every indication is that Elders will follow in the footsteps of C. Everett Koop, the country's only other outspoken doctor to occupy that position. Koop bucked the Reagan administration to read the AIDS epidemic like it was.

Token Gestures

Immediately after the election, Bill Clinton continued to show his support for the gay/lesbian community in token, yet still meaningful, ways. Token because they're more symbolic than anything else; meaningful because no other president has ever made these sorts of symbolic gestures toward the queer community.

Thank-you Note to NGLTF Conference

Clinton sent a thank-you letter to the NGLTF fifth annual Creating Change Conference in Los Angeles, the nation's only skills-building conference for queer activists.

After welcoming folks to the conference and thanking them for the "hard work you have done for the advancement of human rights for gay and lesbian people everywhere," Clinton wrote, "I would also like to take this opportunity to thank everyone of you for your tremendous support during our campaign for change—without your support our victory on November 3rd would not have been possible."

Then he asked for help. (He is, after all, a politician.) "I now ask you again for your help and support in implementing the changes that are needed to get America moving forward once more."

Letter to "Light Up the Night" Sponsors

Clinton also wrote a letter to the folks in Atlanta who sponsor the annual "Light Up the Night" Christmas tree lighting ceremony as a benefit for Project Open Hand, which prepares and delivers meals to people with AIDS (PWAs). According to a report in *Southern Voice* (Dec. 17, 1992), Clinton was invited by a board member to come throw the switch on the tree.

Clinton wrote, "During the campaign that Hillary and I just finished, the problems AIDS causes in our society were impressed on us in many personal and vivid ways. As Governor of Arkansas, my administration worked to stop the misery AIDS causes the people who live with it daily."

Only a politician would have the gall to project such a glossy image about a record that caused so much concern among AIDS and gay/lesbian activists throughout the campaign.

Promising that as president he will have "a special responsibility" to halt the spread of AIDS, Clinton talked about education and research and helping "the companions, parents, and loved ones of those brave PWAs."

He concluded: "I commend the gay and lesbian community of Atlanta for the fine work you are doing tonight. The gay community has taught all of us about kindness, caring and compassion during its fight against AIDS. I have learned from your fight. Your fight will be mine as president."

Hope springs eternal.

Mixner Confident Clinton Will Follow Through

David Mixner feels confident that Bill Clinton will follow through on many of his promises to the queer community.

In a major interview with the *Washington Blade* just after the election, Mixner said that Clinton "has every intention of moving decisively and in a timely manner both on the war against AIDS and the executive order protecting lesbians and gays in federal employment, including the military."

Mixner also thinks Clinton will appoint more out queers to his administration. But any gay or lesbian appointments by Bill Clinton will be scrutinized thoroughly, according to Mixner. "I think that the first few gay and lesbian appointments in this administration will be scrutinized and brutalized almost to the extent that Anita Hill was by the Jesse Helmes, the Alan Simpsons, and the Phil Gramms in the U.S. Senate in any sort of confirmation process. Whoever decides to proceed through such a process better be prepared for an in-depth examination, publicly, of all of their lives, personal, professional, and otherwise."

Playing at the Ball

Populist was the key word for the inaugural events. Everyone was represented: yuppies, queers, blacks, Asians, Latinos, the working-class, the ruling class, the American corporations, big name entertainers, you name it.

Nationally acclaimed black poet Maya Angelou read a poem commissioned for the occasion. Entitled *On the Pulse of the Dawn*, it spoke of how all Americans, from all backgrounds and races, need to:

> *Lift up your eyes upon*
> *This day breaking for you*
> *Give birth again*
> *To the dream.*

Included in the long lists of Americans Angelou mentioned by name were "the gay, the straight, the preacher."

HRCF, NGLTF and the Gay and Lesbian Victory Fund held their own inaugural events, drawing thousands. Popular singer/songwriter Melissa Etheridge came out at the Victory Fund ball. A gay male and a lesbian couple were included in the inaugural parade's American Family float, according to the *Philadelphia Gay News* (January 29-February 4, 1993). NAMES Project volunteers carried 90 panels of the internationally recognized AIDS quilt, which now contains 22,000 hand-made panels from all over the world, the largest memorial to the victims of any disease.

Members of the Gay and Lesbian Bands of America, a group that consists of 23 bands from across the country, performed in the parade. The group now has the distinction of being the first, and we hope not the last, out performers to play at an inauguration.

Lisa Strongin, president of the group, told the *Bay Area Reporter*, "It's a coup to be a part of this event." Strongin also said, "Clearly, we have been included not only because we have shown that we're good, but because we're lesbians and gay men. That's important to the inaugural committee and it says good things for us and for America."

How did they achieve that distinction? They applied for it. No surprise that they were chosen. The choice of a band that plays *Stars and Stripes* and *America the Beautiful* was a safe one. As were the choices for most of the entertainment at the inauguration. Sure, the festivities included more people of color than ever before—but no green-haired anarchists or revolutionary black rap artists. Still, Michael Jackson made a plea for PWAS, and many celebrities wore red ribbons (symbol of support for the fight against AIDS) on their lapels.

One major problem: the affair was financed to the tune of $17 million in loans from corporate America, according to the *New York Times* (January 19, 1993). In other words, Bill Clinton owes corporations big time. What will be the payback? That's the scary part.

Married to Clinton?

Historic is a word you hear a lot these days when it comes to Bill Clinton and the queer community. And if more out queers do get appointed to the administration, which I have every reason to believe they will, the word will pop up even more.

No one's denying that everything about this election is monumental in terms of how involved out queers have been—and inevitably will continue to be.

But our involvement is no longer the issue. Our marriage to the Democrats is now the concern. We courted and were courted by Bill Clinton. We walked down the aisle with him. We looked him in the eyes and, repeating after the Minister of Assimilation, vowed, "We take this man to be our lawfully wedded spouse, to have and to hold, from this day forward, till the end of his term and beyond."

We danced the first dance, shoved the wedding cake in his mouth and tossed the bouquet out into the crowd. Our friends partied with us, threw the rice and tied the cans to the back bumper of the getaway car. We arrived at the honeymoon suite and hung out the Do Not Disturb sign.

It's now the morning after. The bride and groom aren't looking perfect any more in the harsh post-election light. There's a new awkwardness as we try to figure out how to live together happily. The honeymoon is over; real life begins.

A Different Read

Like a bride who realizes that her new husband isn't good in the sack, not everyone is all starry-eyed about the groom. The *New Republic*'s Adam Nagourney had no illusions concerning the man from Little Rock. He draws the bottom line in the magazine's January 4 & 11, 1993 issue: "A midlevel campaign aide, who became more open about his sexuality as the campaign went on—'I was transformed,' he says—still won't be named for this article in case it would complicate his efforts to land a job in the administration. His experience could soon be replicated by many others."

Indeed, when the smoke of the celebrations cleared, Clinton, the great queer rights knight in shining lavender armor, was suddenly thinking of appointing a commission to look into the question of the military ban on queers. He didn't say anything about a commission during the campaign. All he said was that he would issue an executive order eliminating the ban within the first 100 days in office.

Another thing: Bill Clinton's first 27 appointments did not include an AIDS czar. Disquieting given how urgent the appointment of an AIDS czar seemed in his speeches during the election.

Even Bob Hattoy told the *New Republic* that he was concerned about Clinton's post-election performance.

Caution Against Euphoria

Still, the resumes were coming in from gays and lesbians around the country seeking jobs within the new "liberal" administration. HRCF delivered the resumes, in bulk, to the transition team. In fact, HRCF retained the services of a prestigious public relations firm to help activists polish their resumes.

Clinton's aides said early on that the resumes they received were mostly from monied individuals within the queer community. No surprise there.

I think the best comments about Bill Clinton after the honeymoon were expressed by Harry Britt, the gay man who was appointed to the vacant seat on San Francisco's Board of Supervisors after Harvey Milk's murder and who remained on the Board until he retired in January 1992. Britt told the *San Francisco Sentinel* a few weeks after the election, "The generosity and good will of liberals is not what makes us free. Our successes in the 90's will not depend on Bill Clinton, but on how assertive we are."

Even more to the point: "If we decide [Clinton's] the messiah and he's going to take care of us," Britt said, "we're going to get fucked big time."

Said San Francisco activist Bryant Kong, a member of the progressive Green Party, "Everybody's happy that Bush is gone. That's fine. But just because Ronald Reagan and George Bush were horsemen of the Apocalypse doesn't mean that Bill Clinton is the messiah. I think the things we will get out of him are sort of the national policy civil rights—'we're included'—abstract things. There'll be inclusion of lesbians and gays in the national discourse, lesbians and gays in the military might do okay now. ... [As far as] civil rights, we may get some national policy things there. What it boils down to for me is I think people are going to be disappointed. Having the symbolic respect, having the inclusion discourse will do for a while."

Achtenberg seemed to agree with Kong in a *Washington Blade* interview (December 25, 1992). She said of Clinton's pro-gay/lesbian activities: "What they do essentially for most of us in our day-to-day lives is not as significant as the symbol they represent. They sort of give us a national forum to change hearts and minds.

The challenge is to try to figure out how to use the forum."

Even Mixner, in that post-election interview with the *Blade*, said, "I think it's important to keep our expectations in check. I think it's very important to be vigilant."

William Dobbs of New York's Queer Nation and ACT UP echoes this last sentiment. In a *Washington Blade* interview (December 25, 1992), he commented: "Just when you've got somebody who's on your side is when you really push harder, because we're asking for a very big thing, which is to cure AIDS, and it cannot be done without pressure at all levels."

We've come full circle. The ACT UP Presidential Project folks warned us about "Slick Willie" from the beginning. Yet we had to support Clinton, we had no choice. We knew he was educable.

Now it's vital that we realize Bill Clinton's shortcomings and proceed with caution. Slippery road ahead, icy conditions preeminent; drive carefully.

8

Outsiders on the Inside

FIRST A FABLE. Once upon a time in the old days, the gay and lesbian movement was an outsider. It looked on the halls of power and demanded to be let inside. Raising its fist high in the air, it screamed, "We're gonna break down the doors if you don't let us in."

This movement yearned to wield power that would make those inside pay attention to its concerns. So it marched in the streets, lobbied the folks on the inside, and made as much noise as possible. That strategy eventually gained this movement friends on the inside.

Soon, the friends on the inside saw the advantages of including the queers on the outside, so they courted this boisterous movement. They didn't get very far because they served an evil warlock who tied their hands behind their backs and wouldn't let them give away any of the riches of the empire.

A great white father appeared, walking the presidential trail, promising the movement admission to his kingdom, a new kingdom, he said, unlike the one he left behind in the land of rocks and difficult choices. A kingdom that would fly a rainbow flag, the mascot of the queers. Just follow me, he said, and the movement fell in line.

With the support he received, the great white father slew the evil warlock and took over the empire. Doors opened in the halls of power. Keeping his promise, he brought queers inside. So, many of the queers on the outside donned the suits and dresses of the power brokers, stuffed their briefcases full of official papers and rode the buses or drove their cars to jobs in the nation's capital where the great white father now dwelled.

They did the great white father's bidding, and became nice queers, refocusing their anger and their rudeness into the mantra of the party: "The great white father will provide. Trust in him always."

Whenever they doubted the great white father, they repeated this mantra over and over until calm came over them. They hung these words above their desks in proper wooden frames. Before long they didn't have to chant anymore.

It was a new day all over the kingdom.

Harder on the Inside

For the gay and lesbian movement, the election of the great white father is indeed a brand new day. HRCF's Tim McFeeley summed it up perfectly when he said that queers are now "part of the governing coalition." Which means that certain select queers are going to be the folks on the inside, many perhaps occupying the positions of those who were vilified these past two decades for their indifference or their hostility to queers and their issues, especially AIDS.

The change is bound to be traumatic for an outsider movement, one that is not used to the open doors and the conference tables of the insiders.

"It's been easy in a way to be outside the governing

coalition and to just criticize," McFeeley told the *Washington Blade* after the election. "I think it's a much harder job to be part of the governing coalition and to know when to criticize and when to [offer] support." He said that gays and lesbians might have to adopt new strategies for dealing with the change in their status in the new government.

A change that Vaid described as "from pariahs to being welcome partners."

Mixner's take on what queers need to do in terms of this strategy involves understanding that the White House "isn't the be all and end all." Mixner said, "A lot of our work will take place in the agencies, at the cabinet level. I think that it's important to understand that for a number of issues we don't have to call Bill Clinton right away. This can be handled at all sorts of different levels of government. And we will find very friendly, receptive people in those positions."

Provided, of course, that there are indeed "friendly, receptive people" in those levels of government.

No Bed of Roses

Not everyone is so certain that things will be coming up roses in the Clinton years.

Ann Northrop of ACT UP/New York said, "I think we have to continue ... working inside and outside. You offer them a chance to do the right thing. You also deserve the right to yell at them if you don't agree with them."

For Bryant Kong, roses is not something to expect of politicians, even those who ride in recking of the scent. "It boggles my mind," he said, "when I see people go through the same cycle every election of being excited about the latest candidate, or the latest personality, that we're going to get all of these jobs or civil rights or whatever from them. Then finding out that we're the same as before. It's amazes me how much we swallow the lip service."

Early indications are that the great white father may not have a completely new face or scent. Even before he officially moved into the castle on the Potomac, Clinton had already showed frightening signs of mimicking the old warlock: he supported Bush's eleventh hour bombing of Iraq and reversed his campaign position on welcoming Haitian refugees. Not to mention his sudden cold feet on the lifting of the military ban.

Dropping the Bomb

The following would be a fairy tale except that all of the details are true.

Former Philadelphia Mayor Wilson Goode was the first black mayor of the east coast "city of brotherly love" from 1984–1992. He rode into office with the support of the city's sizeable black population, as well as the progressive vote, including a big chunk from the gay/lesbian/bisexual community.

Like Diane Feinstein and Richard Hongisto, he was a self-proclaimed liberal. He was going to do any number of things for the black community. He was going to turn the city around. Yet when folks in a middle-class black neighborhood in West Philadelphia objected to the presence of a radical black, back-to-nature group called MOVE (which didn't believe in bathing or housecleaning or even garbage disposal), police dropped an "incendiary device" (a bomb by any other name) on the MOVE house, killing most of the adults and children inside and burning down several blocks. Hundreds of blacks suddenly found themselves homeless.

It was meant to be an eviction notice—not an obituary.

Did Goode authorize the dropping of that bomb? Hearings into the matter decided "criminal charges were not warranted." Ditto for the police chief, a white man. Ditto for all the public officials involved.

What was most important about this whole affair was that a black mayor was in power, and thus responsible, when this bomb was dropped on that black section of the city to evict a black group, leaving hundreds of black folks homeless.

Will a house full of queers in the Castro find themselves in flames because a gay or lesbian public official wants to serve an eviction notice on a radical back-to-nature faeries group the neighbors don't like?

It's not far-fetched anymore.

Must Guard Against Complacency

Another important question the gay/lesbian movement must ask now is: what becomes of political organizing in the Clinton years?

It's much easier to incite folks when you're an outsider, much easier to mobilize the numbers in the streets, much easier to garner money and resources. When you're on the inside, a complacency can set in that says, "We've arrived, baby. Don't worry. Everything will be solved by the folks inside."

If everything isn't taken care of by the folks inside, will those on the outside forgive those on the inside their shortcomings? Look the other way when they don't come through with their promises? Not hold them accountable for their actions? Tread lightly?

We do that now.

Out queers on the San Francisco Board of Supervisors are treated with kid gloves by the queer media. The attitude seems to be: let's support them because they're all we have. The same can be said for the national queer press and Barney Frank and Gerry Studds.

But our maturation as a movement demands that we not tread lightly anymore, that we learn to call on the carpet when necessary the folks inside who claim to represent us. The folks in the suits and dresses must not deter us from what we as a movement must do in the coming years. If they don't serve the queer community, then those gay/lesbian political appointees should be denounced. Plain and simple. No double standards. No mercy. They are just as accountable as the straight folks.

We've had folks on the inside before. Closeted queers who sometimes helped us, but mostly hindered us. Having alleged queer Pentagon spokesperson Pete Williams and alleged queer NEA head Anne-Imelda Radice on the inside never helped the gay/lesbian/bisexual movement on the military or the NEA front. Not one iota.

Now that NGLTF representatives may be doing brunch with the out queers in the administration to discuss issues of concern, will the bureaucracy respond any differently? It's going to be difficult for the outsiders in this movement to know how to behave as insiders, how to juggle the demands of the great white father with the demands of their own community. It's going to be difficult for those still on the outside after the appointments are made to know exactly how to proceed; how to organize—when necessary—masses of people in the streets. How to convince them that all is not well just because the great white father says it is.

Maintaining the Pressure

Above all else, it's going to be essential to continue the marches, the street actions, the pressure from without— to keep those on the inside on the ball, and to remind Bill Clinton that we can always pull out another ACT UP Presidential Project.

"It's going to be continually frustrating for queers who don't work in the system to have to deal with the queers who are in the mainstream," said activist Kong, who will not get an appointment to the Clinton administration.

My rule is simple. Forget sexual orientation. As with the NEA's Anne-Imelda Radice, whether or not she's a lesbian, and therefore a "sister," is irrelevant. It's what she does and says that counts. Period.

The sexual orientation of the politician may matter as far as queers getting a foot in the door, but it won't matter if gay/lesbian issues aren't addressed or the solutions offered by the appointees aren't satisfactory.

More than ever before, actions must speak louder than words. Allegiances must be drawn not on the basis of who's queer, but on who's doing the work that queers need done.

Traitors—those queers who don't do what they can on gay/lesbian issues—are no better than their heterosexual counterparts. They deserve no mercy from us. Which is what we've said when we outed folks.

Out, Out, Damn Queer

Outing is exposing a closeted person's homosexuality because he or she is using a position of power to betray the gay/lesbian/bisexual community.

At one point ACT UP outed the governor of a midwestern state because he signed several pieces of objectionable AIDS legislation into law. The Pentagon's Pete Williams was outed because he never denounced the military's discrimination against queers.

Outing is about exposing the hypocrisy of queer politicians who perform anti-gay/lesbian actions or become accomplices by their constant silence. As the ACT UP slogan says, "Silence = Death." The silence of the Reagan and Bush administrations on AIDS certainly led to many deaths.

Many in the queer community have serious reservations about outing anyone, even a corrupt anti-gay/lesbian politician. Many in the queer community will object to denouncing or badgering an out gay man or lesbian who doesn't perform to our liking.

It'll be touch-and-go at first. But eventually, I believe, the movement will grow up and realize that we can't afford to protect those who don't look out for their own people.

Crumbs ... or a Piece of the Pie?

Who Bill Clinton chooses as his out queer appointees and where he places them in his administration will determine whether we receive a piece of the pie or mere crumbs. It won't take long to tell whether we're entering this union as an equal partner or as a member of a harem, a mere decoration, another notch on Bill Clinton's worn bed post.

We don't need symbolic appointments; we need a woman like Joycelyn Elders as United States Surgeon General. We need a woman like her in lots of positions. We need folks with guts who have the power to make decisions and move mountains when an injustice needs to be addressed.

We need appointees who are not afraid to challenge the status quo, to risk losing their jobs, to call Bill Clinton himself on the carpet if they have to, in order to help their people.

I don't think that's what we'll get with Bill Clinton.

I don't think Bill Clinton himself is that kind of man. So why would we expect that of his appointments?

What I think we can realistically expect from a great white father like Bill Clinton is a new policy on the military (watered down via a commission, perhaps), an executive order addressing federal employment, and some good AIDS policies, including an increase in funding. We'll also see a liberal appointment to the United States Supreme Court.

A lot more will be garnered from the various departments, as David Mixner pointed out. I'm not talking major reforms here. I'm talking basic civil rights issues. Access to information, a chance to state our case on an issue, to be part of many processes. We'll be visible in the Clinton administration. The country will know we can be trusted in government, that we can be good bureaucrats like everyone else, that we can add to the reams of sometimes meaningless paperwork coming out of the nation's capital every minute of every day.

The United States Justice Department's report on gay teen suicide will certainly be released. The gathering of anti-gay/lesbian violence statistics will proceed more smoothly. Activists will advise on policy matters affecting the gay/lesbian community. Doors will creak open.

The Struggle Isn't Over

Despite these gains, and no matter what this administration does or says, discrimination will continue, bashings will increase (as they have for years now), queer teens will still take their own lives.

The right-wing will continue to organize and attempt the repeal of gay/lesbian rights legislation throughout the country. The GOP may have lost, but remember, the right scored victories in two instances: Colorado and Tampa.

Already, there's talk of anti-gay/lesbian initiatives in other states, including California. The religious right that criticized George Bush for being soft on queers hasn't faded into the woodwork. It's festering beneath the body politic of this country, ready to ooze forth at any moment like the slimy infestation it is.

I have no doubt that statewide initiatives will become the rage of the 90's for these religious bigots. Anything they can do to challenge the rights of gays and lesbians will be done.

Immense Task Ahead

We must pursue every possibility on the AIDS front. Even an AIDS czar or a Manhattan Project will not end the epidemic that has swept this country in the past ten years. Too many years of neglect must be addressed. Restructuring is needed at the National Institute of Health to facilitate research gains. A ban on foreigners with AIDS must be lifted. Discrimination against those with HIV/AIDS—in insurance as well as in other areas—should be addressed without delay.

National health care must become a reality. Not only

because it is a right we should enjoy as citizens of this country, but because it is the only way to handle catastrophic illnesses such as AIDS, something activists have long realized.

Without medical care of some sort, it is impossible to afford AIDS. The high cost of medication (compounded by tremendous greed on the part of pharmaceutical companies) and hospitalization (ditto for the medical establishment) sends so many into poverty. Right now, the burden of the cost is on the public welfare system, which is inadequate to handle the numbers affected by this disease. The result, especially for persons of color, is homelessness and a shorter life expectancy.

National health care is an idea long overdue. It's immoral that the United States does not have it. Even South Africa has it. How can this country call itself civilized and not guarantee health care for all citizens regardless of ability to pay?

I hope Bill Clinton will never be allowed to slither out of tackling this concern. We must force him to be the president who signs the national health care bill.

No Slack for Clinton

I wonder if Bill Clinton realizes the enormity of the task he faces, just in the area of AIDS alone? As the gay and lesbian community realized years ago, AIDS affects every aspect of life in this society—from education to health care to insurance to dating to daily life.

Clinton must give the folks in his administration full reign to do what must be done to address the problem realistically for the first time in a decade. With the recent expansion of the Centers for Disease Control definition of what constitutes AIDS, another 40,000 cases are expected to be added to the body count in 1993.

As of January 1, 1993, 160,000 of the 242,000 Americans diagnosed with AIDS (under the old definition) have died. As of the same date, over 10,000 people have died in San Francisco alone. Grimly sobering numbers.

Though he rode into office expressing the best of intentions on tackling AIDS, the great white father and his administration must be watched every step of the way; he must not be allowed any slack. The country can't afford it.

In exchange for the gay vote, Clinton has bargained for the kind of accountability every politician deserves—never to have peace until justice is done.

9

Gays and the Military

Join the Army. Travel to exotic distant lands; meet exciting, unusual people—and kill them.

Tee-shirt slogan

IF NOTHING ELSE, Bill Clinton will probably go down in history as the president who lifted the ban against gays/lesbians/bisexuals in the military. That ban is derived from Department of Defense Directive 1332.14, section H.1, which has been in effect since 1943. It reads:

Homosexuality is incompatible with military service. The presence in the military environment of persons who engage in homosexual conduct or who, by their statements, demonstrate a propensity to engage in homosexual conduct ... seriously impairs the accomplishments of the military mission. The presence of such members adversely affects the ability of the Armed Forces to maintain discipline, good order, and morale; to foster mutual trust and confidence among service members; to ensure the integrity of the system of rank and command; to facilitate assignment and worldwide deployment of service members who frequently must live and work under close conditions affording minimal privacy; to recruit and retain members of the armed forces; to maintain the public acceptability of military service; and to prevent breaches of security. Homosexual acts are crimes under the Uniform Code of Military Justice.

About 1,500 personnel are dismissed from the various branches of the military each year for being queer. According to a 1992 report by the General Accounting Office entitled Defense Force Management: DOD's Policy on Homosexuality, the U.S. spent $493,195,968 enforcing this policy during the decade 1980–90 (16,919 service members were dismissed). In 1990 alone, $27 million was spent to dismiss more than 1,000 service members.

The report asks Congress to consider removing the ban on queers.

Dismissal on "less than honorable" grounds for being queer means no access to Veterans Administration benefits or the Veterans Administration health-care system. It also means that employers who check into one's military record can use the discharge against the former military person who is gay or lesbian.

During the campaign Bill Clinton promised to issue an executive order within his first 100 days rescinding Directive 1332.14. Such an order would mean that gays/lesbians/bisexuals will be able to serve in the military without hiding their sexual orientation.

As this book goes to press, President Clinton had taken the first steps toward fulfilling that promise: he ordered the military to suspend asking inductees about their sexual orientation. He also put a hold on discharging anyone for being gay. He plans to meet with the military leaders and Congress to formulate an executive order that everyone can live with, and he intends to release that executive order in six months.

Military Establishment Says 'No Way'

Of course, a lot of people in the military establishment aren't keen on such an executive order from President Bill Clinton. Testifying before the House in early 1992, General Colin Powell, then-chair of the Joint Chiefs of Staff, said of gays and lesbians in the armed forces, "I think that's a very difficult problem to give to the military. I think it would be prejudicial to good order and discipline to try to integrate that into the current military structure."

General Powell also said, "It's difficult in a military setting where there is no privacy … to introduce a group of individuals—proud, brave, loyal good Americans, but who favor a homosexual lifestyle—and put them in with heterosexuals who would prefer not to have somebody of the same sex find them sexually attractive."

Powell was quoted weeks later on CNN's *Newsmaker Saturday* program: "Gays now exist in the military, but they are not openly practicing—they're not openly gay. They have not come out of the closet, and that's quite different from them being openly gay."

Clinton agrees that there are gays and lesbians in the military. That's not the issue, he said. "It is whether they can be in the military without lying about it, as long as there is a very strict code of conduct which, if they violate it, would lead to dismissal from the service or other appropriate sanctions."

An unnamed senior Pentagon official admitted to the *New York Times* (November 12, 1992): "There's a huge amount of superstition, hostility and ignorance about what gay people are."

That's an understatement when you consider comments from Admiral Thomas Moorer, former chair of the Joint Chiefs of Staff. Referring to World War II, he told ABC's *This Week With David Brinkley*, "I have been shot down, rescued by ship that was promptly sunk, and then sailed the lifeboats back to Australia, and I shudder to think of the thought of having several lesbians bleeding and homosexuals and so on."

Just as virulent in its hatred of queers is a letter from Jack Black in Kansas City, Missouri, published in the December 14–20, 1992 issue of the *Stars and Stripe—The National Edition*, the country's oldest national veterans' weekly newspaper. The Vietnam vet wrote, "It is one thing to attend college with gays or to work with them in a corporation or government office. In these environments you can disassociate with them after hours. If gays are allowed in the military, all straight people should discourage their children, grandchildren and everyone they know from going into the military."

Any change in military policy towards queers is also opposed by Democratic United States Senator Sam Nunn of Georgia, head of the Armed Services Committee. "We've got to consider not only the rights of homosexuals but all the rights of those who are not homosexual and who give up a great deal of their privacy when they go in the military," he said.

John M. Carney, Commander-in-Chief of the Veterans of Foreign Wars, wrote military service chiefs in support of the current anti-gay/lesbian military policy. "At our 93rd National Convention in Indianapolis this past August [1992], the delegates representing the 2.2-million member VFW passed a resolution opposing homosexual acceptance in the military."

No Evidence of Impairment

It would probably come as a big surprise to Moorer and Black that two Pentagon studies from the 80's found that in the absence of evidence that proves being homosexual would impair one's ability to serve, there should be no discrimination.

The reports, *Pre-Service Adjustment of Homosexual and Heterosexual Military Accessions: Implications for Security Clearance and Suitability,* and *Nonconforming Sexual Orientations and Military Suitability,* were leaked to the press in October 1989.

Interestingly enough, the latter report found that the depth of prejudice against gays and lesbians in the military is "of the same order as the prejudice against blacks in 1948."

In fact, some of the arguments used against gays and lesbians in the military are the same as those used against blacks prior to the 1948 executive order by President Harry Truman that opened the armed forces to African Americans.

In both cases, arguments were made that the morale and efficiency of the military would be reduced. In 1948, Hanson W. Baldwin, then military editor of the *New York Times,* termed the integration of blacks "one of the surest ways to break down the morale of the Army and to destroy its efficiency."

In 1992, Moorer said, concerning the integration of gays and lesbians, "Anything that degrades combat readiness … and capability to fight should not be adopted in my opinion."

Another argument that's familiar to both time periods is that admission of gays and lesbians will cause violence against queers in the military. Says Moorer, "… you're going to have men kissing each other … and the other sailors or soldiers … would see it. … Then, the first thing you would know there would be a fight, and the captain or commander of the unit is going to have to … settle one thing after another."

In 1948, Baldwin wrote of the intermingling of the races in the military, "At best it would cause friction."

A 1941 Navy memo on black service members sounds a lot like the 1943 directive against queers. The memo on blacks reads, in part:

> The close and intimate conditions of life aboard ship, the necessity for the highest possible degree of unity and esprit-de-corps; the requirement of morale—all these demand that nothing be done which may adversely affect the situation. Past experience has shown irrefutably that the enlistment of Negroes (other than for mess attendants) leads to the disruptive and undermining conditions. It should be pointed out in this connection that one of the principal objectives of subversive agents in this country in attempting to break down existing efficient organization is by demanding participation for "minorities" in all aspects of defense.

A Return to Normal After Lifting the Ban

Jim Holobaugh, who was expelled from the ROTC after he came out, thinks that the Clinton executive order will not have drastic effects. "After President Clinton rescinds the military ban on gay personnel, the big news will be how quickly everything returns to normal," he said in a press release announcing the publication of his autobiographical *Torn Allegiances: The Story of a Gay Cadet.*

After he was booted out of the military, the Army demanded that he repay his $35,000 scholarship. But a lot of adverse publicity, including a full-page ad in the *New York Times* signed by 100 college and university presidents challenging the anti-gay policy, prompted the Army to change its mind about the scholarship.

Holobaugh said, "There will not be a mass coming-out of lesbians and gay men in the service. For the most part, those who feel they'd be accepted by their peers are already out. Those who feel they'd be harassed if they came out will remain invisible, even after the policy changes."

Maybe Holobaugh's prediction—that things will return to normal quickly—will come true. In the meantime, according to a report in the *Washington Blade* (January 8, 1992), some queers are "jumping ship" amidst an increasingly hostile atmosphere in the military and the fear that once the ban is lifted they won't be able to use their homosexuality to escape.

Said one unnamed Air Force man, "I hear all kinds of jokes and comments about the fags and how all hell will break loose when Clinton lets them in. It makes you want to crouch into a corner and cower."

The Military: No Safe Space

Contrary to the popular hysteria over gay men attacking straights in the barrack showers, it is gays/lesbians/bisexuals in the military who have never been safe from attack by straights. Civilian queers have also never been safe from America's non-gay military forces.

In October 1992, before the post-election media frenzy over gays/lesbians and the military (it was the lead story in major papers across the country for weeks),

20-year-old sailor Allen Schindler was brutally murdered in Japan by fellow sailors in what is now viewed as
an anti-queer attack.

At the end of January 1993, just after Clinton announced his two-phase plan to end the military discrimination against gays/lesbians/bisexuals, a civilian
gay man was beaten by three marines in front of a gay
bar in Wilmington, North Carolina.

In early February 1993, four sailors and three marines, ages 19–25, were found guilty of assaulting a gay
man in San Francisco's Castro district the year before.

Makes one wonder who is really at risk in the
showers.

Some Support For Lifting the Ban

Oddly enough, despite the Pentagon's negative feelings
about gay and lesbian soldiers being in close quarters
with their heterosexual counterparts, they were not dismissed during the Gulf War. Following the war, an internal military document calling for an end to the policy of
excluding queers was leaked to the public, according to
the *Washington Blade.* Two months later, in response to
a reporter's question, the Department of Defense said
that no "empirical data" exists which "suggests that gays
present a greater risk to the national security than heterosexuals."

Even ultra-conservative William F. Buckley, founder
of *The National Review,* wrote in a syndicated column in
October 1992: "Surely common sense and experience
call for eliminating the discriminatory provisions that
now hypothetically keep gays out of the military and out
of sensitive agencies." While still believing that "homosexuality is a violation of an organic moral code,"

Buckley continued, "There is simply no record of distinctive gay vulnerability in these services to justify categorical, as distinguished from particular, exclusions."

I think that Clinton, his appointed commission or Defense Secretary Aspin will remove the ban. Clinton has no choice at this point except to follow through with a promise he made to queers throughout the campaign. To go back on his word is to show his cowardice.

In addition, polls indicate that the American people favor the lifting of the ban. According to a *Washington Post*-ABC News poll at the beginning of December 1992, 50 percent of those surveyed said that gays and lesbians should be allowed to serve in the military, while 44 percent said that they should not.

Whatever the new president does, the lifting of the ban raises a lot of important issues for the gay/lesbian/bisexual community.

Flashback to Vietnam Era

I attended Bishop Neuman High School in South Philadelphia in the late 60's, at the height of this country's unjust venture into Southeast Asia. Outraged at the daily reports about the war, I used to sneak off to anti-war rallies, avoiding the television cameras because if papa saw me on the evening news there would be hell to pay. Papa was a staunch Republican, a supporter of all that his party did; he expected his famiglia to follow suit.

When I graduated from high school in 1969, I went immediately into college to avoid the draft. Though I knew I was queer, I couldn't use that to avoid the military. How would I explain it to my parents? Besides, I was afraid the draft board would tell my family what I had told them.

A friend, who is also gay, registered as a conscientious objector rather than use his sexual orientation to get out of active duty. I saw the ordeal he endured in trying to convince them that, as a former seminarian and strongly moral person, he was repulsed by the thought of fighting in a war. It certainly discouraged me from going the conscientious objector route. College was an easier choice.

When the first gay soldier went public with his ouster (Sgt. Leonard Matlovich in the mid-70's), I was involved with the gay/lesbian movement in Philadelphia. Though I was a strong civil rights activist, I was perplexed. Why would queers want to be in the military? It's one thing if you're drafted, but to *choose* to go in—! What was going on?

Now, over fifteen years after Matlovich first challenged the military policy of exclusion, I ask the same question when I hear that the lifting of the military ban is a top priority for my community.

Lifting the Ban—Necessary But Not Easy

As a strictly civil libertarian issue, there is no argument: the military policy must go. Bill Clinton should issue his order, and justice will be done. Provided, of course, that some provision is made to equalize benefits programs so that gay and lesbian military personnel can extend their health care and such to their domestic partners.

But this can't be done with a mere stroke of the executive pen. A lot of questions need to be addressed, such as: What about those who have been dismissed? Will the order be retroactive, and if it is, can they get back pay? Clinton has admitted that the executive order is not an easy call.

"How to do it, the mechanics of doing it, I want to consult with military leaders about that," Clinton told the *New York Times.* "There's time to do that. My position is we need everybody in America that's got a contribution to make that's willing to obey the law and work hard and play by the rules."

Aspin, at the press conference announcing his nomination for Defense Secretary, said, "We need to discuss it and work it out among ourselves. But, I think that the word from the top here is to deal with this thing very, very carefully, but to deal with it very, very deliberately. I agree with that policy, and that's what we're going to do."

Serious Question for Gay Community

Bill Clinton will no doubt find a way to issue his executive order, and address every concern he has to address. That leaves the queer community with a serious question: *what are we gaining?* The right to join the military as open gays and lesbians and work for the Pentagon in enforcing oppressive policies throughout the world?

As a pacifist, I have a problem with war in general. Politically, I do not agree with America's military policies, policies that involve supporting pro-American dictators and protecting the money interest of this country's multinational corporations.

With a stroke of Bill Clinton's mighty hand—we, too, can go to the Middle East and kill for America's oil companies when another Gulf War breaks out. We, too, can be sent to places like Vietnam to fight off the godless commies. We, too, can be used to help put dictators in power in Latin America. Is that what we want?

Place of Refuge

The military's slick "Be all you can be" ads stress the job skills and the opportunities afforded those who enlist. To look at the ads, you'd think joining the new squeaky clean armed forces was no more dangerous than working in the financial district of any American city. The military now offers status, self-esteem, a decent paying job, and a chance to travel.

As a result, the military has become a place of refuge for the working class, especially people of color, who have no other job opportunities, who want relief from poverty and lives of hopelessness. What a deal—obtain an education, learn computer programming, get free room and board, kill people.

I'm not laying the blame on the working class or gays and lesbians who take advantage of the military. They're not the villains.

Condemn the Institution

As activist Kong said, "In terms of queer people who are in the military now, or who want to be in the military or who, because they're poor or black, don't have much option except to get a nice life for themselves in the military, I don't think those people should be penalized through a rigid theorization of the military as bad.

"You need to allow people to live their lives, especially with the limited choices most people have, while the systematic reform is taking place and while you're demilitarizing the economy."

In other words, condemn the institution without condemning those who work within it.

It's easy enough to see that the culprit is not the individual who joins, but the militarization of our economy. Better jobs are available in or with the armed forces. No other institution in this society has that kind of budget.

Politicians feel the effects of this militarization of our economy all the time. Not only are they lobbied by the fat cats at the Pentagon, but they have to fight the closing of defense plants and naval yards because so many of their constituents are employed there. Forget their own feelings about the military. People's livelihoods are on the line.

Now that the working class has become fodder for the military machine, pawns in a power game waged by generals in their safe ivory towers far from the bloodshed, are queers next?

Think about it. A young gay man in some small town in the Midwest, just out of high school and afraid of telling his parents about his sexual identity, opts for the new queers-r-us Army. Now instead of becoming a hairdresser, he can be a butcher.

Some progress!

Some Positive Effects

It's fine to ask Bill Clinton for an executive order to address a basic civil-rights concern. Allowing gays and lesbians into the service may also have a positive effect throughout society, legitimizing us in one more way. If we're good enough to kill for America, we should have civil rights, too.

Another positive effect: The millions of straight recruits and personnel in the service get to interact with out queers and see that we're flesh and blood human beings. Many of these heterosexual service members will take positive attitudes about queers home with them.

Not a Progressive Move

But the advantages of such a policy don't outweigh the disadvantages. I wonder how many of our leaders have really thought through all the implications of what they want Clinton to do. The queer movement cannot act in isolation of other movements—particularly those that oppose the military's policies throughout the world.

Asking for admission into the military is not a progressive move. It aligns us with regressive forces, those that refuse to see the problems of America for what they are. And the military is part of America's problem right now.

The military's budget is a problem, taking away much needed financial resources that could go into social programs; the military mentality is a problem, allowing the government to live out macho control fantasies throughout the world. As long as the military exists, especially on such a large scale, this country will never become a true force for peace in the world. As long as we can fall back on bullying people with our military might, we will never learn peacemaking skills.

The military can cope with queers in its rank, just as it coped with blacks. There will be no discipline problems, no breakdown of morale. The military will go on—and that's the unfortunate part.

Asking Bill Clinton to lift the military ban is a case of politics making very strange bedfellows.

Promoting Peace

As far as I am concerned, the queer movement should be aligned with the anti-military efforts. We need to be out on the front lines against intervention in the affairs of other countries, against the use of military force, against invasions and coupes and takeovers, against defending oil interests in the Middle East with bombing raids.

Two years ago, NGLTF came out against Bush's bombing of Iraq. It was a courageous act for a mainstream gay/lesbian/bisexual organization. It sent the right message: queers oppose military intervention for profits; queers are on the progressive side.

It was painful to hear at the same time that Miriam Ben-Shalom, a lesbian ousted from the Army, asked George Bush to send a lavender brigade over to the Middle East to fight the "good fight."

Instead of wanting in on the military, we should be advocating for non-military jobs that promote peace and train people to overcome poverty and despair. Why not put people to work in this country helping to rebuild our cities and feed the hungry? Channel some of that defense budget into social welfare programs that can be staffed by the same young men who now pursue Uncle Sam for a job. This is where queers should align themselves.

Instead, we're stuck arguing with the Neanderthals in the Department of Defense and the religious right that queers will make good soldiers. We look to the studies, done by the military itself, that prove how obedient and loyal we can be. Look, queers can kill, too; look, queers can defend oil interests. Look, queers can be fodder.

No Party Dress

When Clinton issues his order, I won't get out my party dress. I'm sure thousands of queers and their supporters will fill Castro Street that night, to mark what they see as an historic moment, the marriage of the queer community with the forces of imperialism. I'm sure gay and lesbian leaders will have lots of good quotes for the mainstream press.

I wonder how many of these leaders will express reservations about lifting the ban. I wonder how many will use the opportunity to express outrage at the military itself and the policies of this country in other lands. I wonder how many will make the distinction between the gay/lesbian civil liberties issue, the issue of the rights of individuals to choose the military, and the greater one of this country's horrendous military policies.

I'll be cringing in my apartment that night, shuddering at the thought that the next time we go off on some unjust battle somewhere—as inevitably we will, even under the former anti-war activist Bill Clinton—out gays and lesbians will be in the ranks, ready to obey whatever order they receive from homophobic men like Admiral Thomas Moorer.

A stranger marriage of convenience there has never been.

10

Where Do We Go From Here?

DOROTHY AND HER HAPLESS FRIENDS merrily strode off to Oz, convinced that the wizard who lived in the Emerald City would give them what they needed to be happy in life. And all would be well forever more.

Many in the queer community skipped down the same yellow brick road in search of Bill Clinton, the wizard who would set things right again, who would give us a brain, a heart, whatever we needed to be whole. All we had to bring to him was the broomstick of the Wicked Witch, George Bush. We delivered it in style.

After 12 years of Reagan/Bush politics, who could blame us for looking to any Democrat for salvation, no matter how many buttons he pushed behind the curtain or how much smoke he conjured up to impress us? As the smoke clears, we must remember that the wizard's words to Dorothy are true for us, as well: we have the power within us to do whatever we want.

The question is: *What do we want now?* A long-term alliance with the Democrats? The election of more of our own to political office? Federal gay/lesbian rights legislation? The right to serve in the military?

I see lots of trouble ahead if we don't take stock of ourselves right now, if we don't look at where we're heading. If we don't demand more than a federal rights bill, a ban on military discrimination, and adequate funding for AIDS.

The System: Only Part of the Answer

It all comes down to this: Will we put all of our energy into working within the system, or will we explore and open other routes to achieving our agenda? Will we put all our stock in Bill Clinton or look at other possibilities—the Green Party, Socialism, a queer party?

As I see it, working within the system is problematic. You have to make so many compromises. You try to serve your constituency, represent the place and the people you come from, but the boys in power and the boys with the money want your loyalty above all else.

Sometimes, to truly serve your community, you have to ruffle a lot of power-broker feathers. How many of us have the guts to do that? Not many folks, from where I stand. That's why it's almost impossible to be an idealist in American politics today.

Harvey Milk ruffled a lot of feathers by insisting that we could defeat the Briggs Initiative, by insisting we could have a piece of the pie, if we wanted it. The man had guts. And he died for it.

Milk knew that we have to work within the system. We have to pursue politicians and political office and electoral gains. But it's obvious that any gains realized from working within are stop-gap measures, not self-sufficient long-term solutions. Working within the system—winning friends and gaining influence—is only part of the answer. There's other important work to do.

A Look At Where We Came From

The gay/lesbian liberation movement was born in the fiery embers of a riot against the New York City police, who raided the Stonewall Inn in June 1969. Police routinely raided the Big Apple's gay bars in the 60's, but this night was different: drag queens, with the least to lose since they are often denigrated within the queer community itself, fought back, literally trapping officers inside the bar, as they pelted it with stones and whatever else they could find to throw.

The gay/lesbian liberation movement that sprang up overnight after those three days of rioting in Greenwich Village replaced the homophile groups of the 50's and 60's The homophiles, radical in their day just because of what they were, were dinosaurs by that hot summer night in 1969, especially in light of their counterparts in the anti-war, civil rights and women's struggles. Face it, by 1969 the kids in the trenches of the anti-war movement were robbing banks and helping draft dodgers across the border into Canada.

Yet, of all the fronts, the gay/lesbian liberation movement made America the most uneasy. There was no way America was going to willingly assimilate these self-styled revolutionary groups that challenged the country's most sacred concepts of gender and sexuality. America the melting pot wasn't even going to simmer for this crowd.

That early group of radicals included drag queens, sado-masochism folks, hippies, civil rights activists, anti-war agitators, and so forth. Not many respectable types—you know, the Marvin Liebmans and Roberta Achtenbergs, the kind it's difficult not to like. The kind you can take home to the family.

Move Toward Assimilation

It turns out that America didn't have to lift a finger to assimilate the queers, because the gay liberation movement generated an assimilationist trend that did the job better than anyone else ever could. The move toward assimilation was not difficult: by the mid-70's gay Democratic clubs and gay chapters of mainstream religious groups were begging society, "Please, accept us, bless us with your holy legitimacy, bestow on us your seal of approval."

Don't get me wrong. There is nothing intrinsically wrong with being part of the establishment, about aspiring to be like the straight white folks next door. It's expected that some queers, like some members of every other disenfranchised group in America, will assimilate: they will have the house in the suburbs with the white picket fence, the dog in the yard, the car in the garage and the bills piled up to their wazoos. And few neighbors will blink an eye about the fact that they're two people of the same sex. They'll even bake goodies for the local protestant church and worry about the waxy buildup on the kitchen floor.

Assimilation for Whites Only

Of course, this applies only if you're white and queer. Queers of color have the added burden of dealing with racism, which exists within the gay/lesbian community as well. Indeed, the queer community has all of the same *isms* of the heterosexual world.

While queers of color may be accepted as gays and lesbians in the mainstream world, they may still be excluded because of their skin color. So this assimilationist trend toward the house in the suburbs is primarily white because whites are the ones middle America will embrace first. And whites have more of the economic means at their disposal to get the house in the 'burbs.'

The Face We Present to the World

It's obvious that white gays and lesbians are more accepted by the mainstream culture than gays and lesbians of color. Look at the talk shows. Queers are the darlings of the talk show circuit—everyone from Geraldo to Oprah to Joan Rivers has queers as guests. From dazzling transvestites to ordinary looking gay or lesbian couples with two-point-eight kids. But did you ever notice how consistently white these guests are? You can probably count on one hand the number of gay people of color who appear on these shows.

What about the queers who speak for our movement in the newspapers, at colleges, in political meetings, on the floor of the Democratic Convention? How many are non-white?

Ditto for the gay/lesbian characters on the sitcoms and the soaps. We hail the progress television has made, but the fact is that as far as queers of color are concerned, the media is still back in pre-history. And that's true even if you count the two gay men on the program *In Living Color.* Hardly revolutionary depictions of black gay men.

Years ago the movement abandoned the use of the word gay because it had become synonymous with male. Now public perception is that it not only means male, it also means white. And whose fault is it? Whites must step aside from power positions in favor of persons of color, queer groups must initiate affirmative action, and gay/lesbian outreach must be done to communities of color.

Not a Truly Multicultural Movement

The gay/lesbian movement has failed to become a broad-based multicultural one, despite claims that it is.

I remember the early days of the AIDS struggle in Philadelphia. The men who started the first local AIDS organization knew how to reach the white gay men who partied in the gay areas of the city; they knew how to contact the white contributors. They knew how to build a white organization from scratch.

A few years later, when faced with charges that the organization was racist, they threw their hands in the air in bewilderment. I truly believe they didn't know how in the world to outreach blacks, Puerto Ricans (the city has a large Puerto Rican population) or Asians. Of course racism may have compounded it. But many whites genuinely don't think of the world as multicultural. The world is America, which equals European, which equals white.

I've run into white queers who think that by declaring their group multicultural, people of color should flock to it. It takes more than a declaration to make a group multicultural. It takes a commitment to multiculturalism on all levels.

If I am Native American and queer, how can I identify with a movement that schedules a Coming Out Day celebration in Sacramento on the same day that my people plan a massive march in San Francisco against the Quincentennial of Columbus' invasion of America?

If I am Jewish and the gay/lesbian movement schedules events on my holy days, why should I go? Why would I care about that movement when it shows no respect for me?

If I am black and I have to enter a room full of otherwise white faces week after week, why would I go back?

Politically Correct

Often times the people who support inclusiveness—who insist on quotas and on the equal participation of women and people of color—are accused of being "politically correct," a phrase that has become anathema for many in the queer community. Political correctness, especially in the eyes of the major media these days, has become a catch-phrase for fascism, for forced integration of groups, for quotas.

Even Bill Clinton, under attack for not appointing enough women to his new administration, talked about feminists wanting quotas as if it were the worst thing that could happen. It's as if he were thinking, "Oh, those politically correct feminists are at it again!"

Often, we do need quotas. Sometimes the only way to change the color of a room or an organization or a movement is to force integration, affirmative action. The idea of the politically correct grew out of a need for more inclusion, to be aware of issues such as race, age, gender, disability. It's a mark of success that political correctness has been trashed in the mainstream press. It's obviously having some affect.

We Are Everywhere

No group representing the queer community can be white only. Or men only. The queer community cuts across all racial, social, economic, class, gender, color, religious, age lines. We have a slogan: *We are everywhere.* It's true. But most people don't think about what that really means.

We are in Chinatown, we are in the Barrio, we are in Little Italy, the WASP suburbs, the black community, among the disadvantaged, the homeless—everywhere. We are the same and we are different. The same because we are gays and lesbians. Different because our needs are divergent. What I need as a Southern Italiano living in the Castro is not the same as what an immigrant Filipino or a poor black or white person needs.

I don't see that distinction being made. I hear monolithic statements made about our needs as gays and lesbians, which come from white gays/lesbians. But our needs are not monolithic.

A Poor Gay? Are You Crazy?

Case in point: Nowhere does the NGLTF transition document mention poverty, homelessness, racism. Nowhere do we get the impression that gay men and lesbians in this country go without food, shelter, clothing, or heat. Why not?

For many queers of color, the basic necessities are essential concerns. Before they can have the privilege of worrying about executive orders on anything, they must eat, keep warm, pay the rent.

White middle-class folks—men and women—forget the fact that not everyone in this society has the luxury of organizing around theoretical issues. Not everyone has been to college, read the academic studies on homosexuality, found a decent paying job. Not everyone belongs to a gym or can afford to buy their goods in the trendy shops in the Castro.

This movement needs to address that in a big way. We need to stop acting as if we are a monolithic white bourgeois population that can easily organize $1,000/ plate fundraisers for politicians.

Or spend hundreds of dollars in plane fare to go to D.C. for a national march.

We are as much a part of the poor and underprivileged in this country—the hungry, the homeless, the illiterate—as any other group. It will be tragic if our agenda does not acknowledges this.

Paris Burns, Leaders Haggle

Do you realize that Paris is indeed burning while gay/ lesbian leaders haggle for crumbs in the back rooms with the politicians?

The poor black and Latino queens depicted in the documentary *Paris Is Burning* are on the outside of this gay/lesbian world of electoral politics and disposable incomes. They're not counted in the "gay" voting precincts or asked their opinions about federal gay/lesbian rights bills.

They find their sense of self-worth not in electing presidents or members of the board of supervisors, but in dressing in drag and parading around in front of judges, often mimicking the upwardly mobile white folks they see in the media or in magazines like *Vogue* and GQ. They find their skin color or ethnic heritage to be a detriment to acceptance in the broader queer community. They find their community in houses, groups of people who live together and support one another because they have only each other.

No one's ever asked them what they need. Their answer might surprise us.

What Do They Need?

I interviewed some homeless folks for a piece I did in *Bay Times* recently on a voucher program started by the Castro/Upper Market Business Association in San Francisco. The program operates like this: A citizen buys a twenty-five cent voucher, gives it to a person on the street who then cashes it in at designated stores in the Castro for food, toiletries, and so forth.

While the program is targeted at the homeless, it doesn't do anything to get people off the street. It wasn't intended to. It was designed to tackle the problem of aggressive panhandling.

One homeless man said to me, "Give me a job." Another said he'd rather have food stamps. Clearly, no one ever thought to ask them what they need. When liberals do things to ease their own consciences, their actions are not always helpful.

We need to listen to the gay folks in Harlem and Southeast L.A. What are they saying to us? Is Bill Clinton going to make a difference for them? Is the NGLTF transition document going to mean a hill of beans to them? What about the March on Washington? When that march is through, when Clinton accepts or rejects the transition document, they'll still have the same poverty to face, the same hopelessness.

The millions we spend on that march could feed a lot of people or go for affordable housing in ghettos like the Castro or Greenwich Village. We don't need to impress Bill Clinton by gathering a million people to D.C. At least not if he's already our friend, as the leadership of the queer community says that he is.

But it's certainly time we let him know that our people need housing and food. And that when he tackles poverty, which he'd better do, he's also helping members of our community.

Problems Don't Sell in Politics

The difficulty is that talking about poverty and homelessness won't sell in the political circles we want to influence. It won't buy us votes the way million dollar fundraisers at posh hotels do. It won't secure ads for our gay/lesbian press.

So many people were thrilled when the *Wall Street Journal* took a look at the financial clout, the disposable income of the gay/lesbian community (in reality, the white gay male community). The paper concluded that we as a community have a lot of extra income to spend on vacations and Madison Avenue gizmos. Oh joy, a new market for corporate America to exploit.

Indeed, an analyst quoted in the article said about gay and lesbian households: "You're talking about two people with good jobs, lots of money, and no dependents. This is a dream market."

I didn't hear a public outcry from gay/lesbian leaders when this article was published. I didn't hear anyone in the queer movement asking for qualifiers on the rosy picture it painted of our community.

These gays/lesbians knew that an article like this in a major mainstream paper would win friends and influence others; it would sell politicians on our agenda and advertisers on our publications; it would legitimatize us in the eyes of a white America that is impressed by money.

The sad fact is that the image this article and others

like it create is of a community that does not include poor whites or blacks, or Latinos, or Asians, or Native Americans. It describes a sub-set community that is white, upwardly mobile and overly consumer-oriented. The perfect marketplace for corporate America.

It's the same image of gay men we saw in the movies *Longtime Companion, Making Love,* and many other Hollywood productions. Even television's *An Early Frost* played into this idea that all gay men are white and bourgeois.

Affluence Used Against Us

This notion of the gay community as affluent is not always an asset. Fundies love to use the fact that we supposedly make more than other disenfranchised groups to prove that we are a "rich class" that doesn't need what they love to call "special rights."

Here's an excerpt from a chart the fundies use to compare "our" income to that of blacks, Latinos and others in the society. The chart was published in *Freedom Journal,* a newsletter of the Oregon Citizens Alliance (OCA), the folks who gave us Measure 9:

	Homosexuals	Nat'l Average	Blacks	Latinos
Average Annual Household Income	$55,430	32,144	12,166	17,939

SOURCES FOR THE FIGURES, ACCORDING TO THE OCA: THE *WALL STREET JOURNAL,* THE "1991 U.S. STATISTICAL ABSTRACT," COLORADO FOR FAMILY VALUES (THE GROUP THAT PASSED THE ANTI-GAY LAW THERE), AND THE *SAN FRANCISCO CHRONICLE.*

I'm not giving credence to the OCA statistics. It is ironic, however, that every category they place next to gays also includes a portion of our community. We are in the black and Latino communities, as well as the national average (some of us are closeted). And some of us who aren't black or Latino are earning the lower incomes listed under those designations.

Clearly, emphasizing our disposal income is to unsheathe a double-edge sword. It's easy to be hurt by that weapon. And by showing such a white bourgeois face, the queer movement in America slits its own throat.

The Long-Range Agenda

Another real danger for gays and lesbians in the post-Clinton victory era is complacency. Many of us think we can pack up and retire because we've elected Bill Clinton, that all is going to be well, especially if he removes the ban on queers in the military and increases AIDS money.

But even if we gain an end to military discrimination and achieve a federal gay rights bill and adequate AIDS funding, we still have only scratched the surface of what needs to be done in this country in order to right the wrongs done us, all of us.

Bill Clinton cannot do our work for us. He can help us by providing relief, give us the means to begin dressing some old wounds. But we have to push forward with our long-range agenda—to aid in the greater struggle for a better society, both within the borders of our own community and in the society-at-large.

People who look to federal rights bills and executive orders as the end-all of our struggle are not only ignoring the needs of many of us who are not white, but also failing to understand history.

The Bottom Line

The passage of the Civil Rights Act nearly 30 years ago did not end racism against African Americans; the Supreme Court decision desegregating the public schools did not put an end to an inferior education for blacks; treaties between Native Americans and the conquerors of this land have not guaranteed the indigenous peoples a quality life; state Equal Rights Amendments did not put women on an equal footing with men, even in terms of what they get paid; reparations to the Japanese for their internment during World War II has not ended Japan-bashing.

A federal gay/lesbian rights bill will not stop teens from being beaten in schools every day. It will not stop lesbians from being raped, murdered or robbed of their children. It will not stop a queer of color from being turned away because of his/her skin color or ethnic heritage—even in the gay/lesbian community. It will not end homelessness in any of the queer neighborhoods in this country, poverty in the Tenderloin area of San Francisco where many queers reside, hopelessness in the lives of those queers who don't have the disposable incomes the *Wall Street Journal* (and the gay/lesbian press) loves to attribute to gay men.

That's the bottom line.

What Do We Want the Movement to Be?

I am hopeful that the next four years will see an end to many of the cruelties of the Reagan/Bush years. I also hope for the emergence of a mass queer movement for real change in this country, a movement that sees as much victory in finding jobs and affordable housing for the homeless in our communities as it does in $1,000/ plate dinners for politicians.

Reject the Status Quo

I'm an old-style liberationist. I'm not looking to be accepted as one of the fold. I don't want legitimacy in an anglo-dominated society that, among other things, is owned by a few families and multinational corporations; that promotes racism, sexism, ageism and other forms of inequality; that wages war against other countries with a budget that could feed every starving person on the planet; that doesn't provide health care to its citizens; that doesn't guarantee the basic survival needs of a human being (food, clothing, shelter, heat, water) upon birth; and that speaks of multiculturalism but has never had a president or color and has comparatively few non-whites in any political office.

I'm not looking to be a member of a mainstream church; married by the state; serve in the military; employed by Dow or General Motors or IBM or Lockheed; or approved for credit.

Work For Change

It's not enough for queers to be integrated into a society that is ripe with ills. We must work to heal those ills. I want to be part of a queer community that is no longer white-dominated or male-dominated; that actively works against racism, sexism, ageism. A community that understands its natural ally is not corporate America or any one political party, but the masses of oppressed peoples of color and the working class. A community that defines progress as more than opening trendy shops in the Castro or staging marches on Washington or raising millions for straight politicians.

I want to be part of a movement that sets agendas based on the needs of people of all colors; a movement that embraces the needy in our midst.

I hope for an end to the Pentagon; an end to the unequal distribution of wealth; an end to poverty, homelessness, racism, sexism, ageism; an end to hunger; an end to religion, an end to ownership of land, people, lovers.

As sexual outlaws in the eyes of America, we have an excellent vantage point. We can either use it to decry the immorality of this country, or we can ignore it and ask for our crumbs. We can use it to guarantee that all of our sisters and brothers are fed, clothed, housed, safe, healthy, and earning a decent wage. We can create neighborhoods that truly welcome all of us—regardless of race, color, religion, gender, or sexual orientation.

We can create work environment that don't exploit. We can explore alternatives like worker-owned enterprises and collectives rather than the traditional capitalist ones.

Right-wing Challenges in the 90's

In the 90's, the gay/lesbian/bisexual movement will face constant initiative challenges to queer rights laws. The right-wing has found its forte—using ignorance and hate to repeal hard-earned rights laws that barely scratch the surface of addressing the needs of the queer community.

The fight against the right-wing in the next decade will cost the queer community more than it can afford in time, energy and money. But I'm confident that we will triumph, as good must, because as humans evolve past the hatred that gave us a history strewn with bloodshed, we will understand the beauty of our diversity.

That fight will be won only if the queer community presents a united and inclusive front—utilizing the resources of all segments, all racial and ethnic groups, all religious denominations, all genders, classes, ages and abilities. A front that forms its alliances with others engaged in the progressive struggle to change America into a truly humane country.

United Through the AIDS Crisis

As a community, gays, lesbians, bisexuals and the transgendered proved that, in a time of crisis, we can be counted on to care for our own when the world wants us to disappear. The onslaught of AIDS forced us to unite in a way we never had before.

The decade ahead demands that we pull together in another way—across all lines, racial, social, economic, age, gender—to fight the menace that lurks in the right-wing, and to fulfill our destiny as a multicultural community. Like America itself, we are the true tossed salad representing every diverse piece of humanity in the world.

True Measure of Progress

For queers, the true measure of progress in this decade will not be in how many political appointments we accrue or how many rights bills we pass. It will not even be in how much respectability we gain. It will be in how well we redefine ourselves as an inclusive, truly multi-cultural community with the strength to act on our convictions.

Dorothy discovered the power within herself to go home again when she clicked her heels together. It's time for us to click our collective heels, to discover the vision and strength within ourselves to forge a better future.